GENERATIONAL CURSES

AND HOW TO BE FREE FROM THEM

GENERATIONAL CURSES

AND HOW TO BE FREE FROM THEM

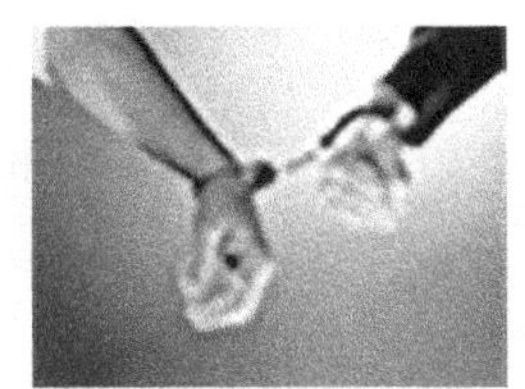

by

Prophetess Jackie Harewood

Published by:

McDougal & Associates
18896 Greenwell Springs RD
Greenwell Springs, LA 70739
www.thepublishedword.com

McDougal & Associates is dedicated to the spreading of the Gospel of Jesus Christ to as many people as possible in the shortest time possible.

ISBN 978-1-940461-79-3

Printed in the US, the UK and Australia
For Worldwide Distribution

DEDICATION

This work is dedicated to the loving memory of my mother, Mrs. Gladys Young, and my father, Lloyd Young, both now in Heaven. Mom, you sat and watched me for months as I worked on this book. You left us in January, and I finally completed the book ten months later. You are no longer with us, but I am sure you and Dad have had a long-awaited reunion. I will always love you both, and you will always be in my heart. Thank you for gracing me with your support and love. I have accepted and am enforcing my generational blessings.

Don't give the devil any opportunity to work.

Ephesians 4:27, GW

CONTENTS

INTRODUCTION

Some might ask, "Why write a book on generational curses and blessings?" Well, are you living up to the level of your inner vision and potential? Personally, I would have to answer, "No, I am clearly not." And why is that? We all start out with big dreams and visions for our future, but when the future finally becomes the present, it rarely lives up to the magnitude of our original dreams. Like many of my generation, I believe that God called me to do great things, to have great influence and to change our world. But we're not there yet. So, what has been holding us back?

I have become convinced that there are many people living under bondages they are not personally responsible for. Looking back to our family tree, we may find that a family member from the past opened doors to certain behaviors and ushered them into the whole family. Thus, some of your behavior, technically, is not your fault. It is time to consider the issue of generational curses.

Beyond generational curses, there are generational blessings. The greatest heritage you can leave for your family is a spiritual heritage that opens up fountains of blessing to each of them. I trust that this book will help many understand better both generational curses and blessings.

Jackie Harewood
Baton Rouge, Louisiana

Chapter 1

THE EXISTENCE OF ANCESTRAL, OR GENERATIONAL, CURSES

Exodus 34:7

Keeping mercy for thousands, forgiving iniquity and transgression and sin, and that will by no means clear the guilty; visiting the iniquity of the fathers upon the children, and upon the children's children, unto the third and to the fourth generation.

Have you ever seen a family in which the father had a problem with uncontrollable anger? Chances are his son or daughter may have the same anger problem. If you look further into their history, you will find that the grandfather or grandmother may have had the problem too.

Have you noticed that you not only suffer with persistent and unreasonable fears or depression, but that your mother and/or father also suffered the same? As noted at the outset, there are many people today who are living under bondages they are not personally responsible for. Some family member from the past opened doors that ushered certain behaviors into the entire family. Thus, some of your behavior, technically, was not initiated by you personally.

There is a controversy over ancestral curses, also known as generational curses. This text is intended to bring to your knowledge the possibility that ancestral curses may be active in your life. Let me say up front: I do *not* believe that you can use this argument of ancestral curses to excuse bad behavior. God expects each of us to take full responsibility for our actions.

There are, however, schools of thought that use this Exodus passage as an argument to prove that we are visited by our forefather's actions. Even more support for this argument can be found in Lamentations:

Lamentations 5:7

Our fathers have sinned and are not; and we have borne their iniquities.

In all fairness, I must admit, that in some situations at least, learned and acquired behavior patterns are responsible for our behavior. However, I want to address behaviors that go beyond learned behavior patterns and border on family tree evidence. Many children come to be disorganized because their parents were disorganized before them. This might be a spiritual bondage that has passed down from one generation to the next.

An ancestral curse is a continual negative behavioral pattern handed down from generation to generation. Interestingly enough, in cases where a person has been adopted and has not had physical or emotional influence from their birth family, they still often end up with the characteristics of their birth family. It has been proven that children don't have to live with their birth parents to learn how they behaved. This means they have inherited behaviors, and these often bring them into spiritual bondage.

The Free Dictionary defines *heredity* as "the genetic transmission of characteristics from parent to offspring. The sum of characteristics and associated potentialities transmitted genetically to an individual organism." [1]

1. http://www.thefreedictionary.com/Inherited+trait

An inherited trait, then, is a characteristic passed from parents to their children. Physical traits are characteristics such as eye color, height and athletic ability. Emotional traits are characteristics such as personality. And social traits are characteristics such as behavior.

Whatever the case, the price for ancestral curses has been paid and the good news is that once you accept Jesus as your Savior, the transference of ancestral curses can stop right there. This, however, is not automatically enforced. The legal right to be free of a curse now exists, but you must walk in that right and make it your own. Spiritually, the potential is there, but it must be appropriated.

Through Christ, you can break any connection you have with ancestral bondages and no longer transmit those bondages to generations to come. Because Christ was made a curse for us, we can be freed from all curses that occur, both as a result of our own sins and also those of our forefathers:

Galatians 3:13

Christ hath redeemed us from the curse of the law,

being made a curse for us: for it is written, cursed is everyone that hangeth on a tree.

Once you become a child of God, technically, the sins of your forefathers can no longer cause curses to be transferred into your life. But you must acknowledge any curse that is already there and repent of it, in order to qualify for freedom from it:

Jeremiah 31:29-30

In those days they shall say no more, The fathers have eaten a sour grape, and the children's teeth are set on edge. But everyone shall die for his own iniquity: every man that eateth the sour grape, his teeth shall be set on edge.

According to Jeremiah, we no longer need to be subject to the behaviors of our fathers. If that is true, then why are there so many believers who seem to be living under ancestral curses? In your own life, was there some bondage that was passed down before you came into covenant with Christ? Was there some legal ground that gave the curse access to your life before you yielded yourself to the Lord? Whatever gave that curse legal grounds was certainly paid for on the cross, and, therefore, its power has been broken. So, what's going on then? It seems that the spirit that gained entrance with the curse is somehow left behind.

When a curse comes upon someone, there is a spirit attached to that curse which brings the curse to the intended recipient. After you accept the blood of Jesus, your sins are forgiven, but the spirit or spirits that brought that curse must be cast out. So the only thing left to do is cast out any spirits that have gained entrance to your life before you accepted Jesus. Then you can be free.

Even after Jeremiah 31 made it clear that believers are redeemed from generational curses, in that very next chapter God mentions again that He will show lovingkindness and He, again, references the same idea:

Jeremiah 32:18, GW

You show mercy to thousands of generations. However, you punish children for the wickedness of their parents. You, God, are great and mighty. Your name is the Lord of Armies.

Ezekiel spoke of this problem:

Ezekiel 18:1-9, GW

The LORD spoke his word to me. He said, "What do you mean when you use this proverb about the land of Israel: 'Fathers have eaten sour grapes, and their children's teeth are set on edge'? As I live, declares the Almighty LORD, you will no longer use this proverb in Israel. The life of every person belongs to me. Fathers and their children belong to me. The person who sins will die.

"Suppose a righteous person does what is fair and right. He doesn't eat at the illegal mountain worship sites or look for help from the idols of the nation of Israel. He doesn't dishonor his neighbor's wife or have sexual intercourse with a woman while she is having her period. He doesn't oppress anyone. He returns what a borrower gives him as security for a loan. He doesn't rob anyone. He gives food to people who are hungry, and he gives clothes to those who are naked. He doesn't lend money for interest or make an excessive profit.

He refuses to do evil things, and he judges everyone fairly. He lives by my rules and obeys my laws faithfully. This person is righteous. He will certainly live," declares the Almighty LORD.

Clearly there are some important concepts here that we all need to learn if we are to live free of the curses of the past.

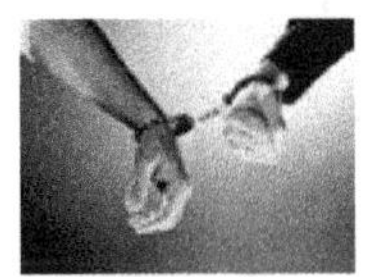

CHAPTER 2

HOW CHILDREN ARE AFFECTED BY CURSES

Mark 9:17-18

And one of the multitude answered and said, Master, I have brought unto thee my son, which hath a dumb spirit; and wheresoever he taketh him, he teareth him: and he foameth, and gnasheth with his teeth, and pineth away: and I spake to thy disciples that they should cast him out; and they could not.

In the movie, "Forrest Gump" (1994), Mrs. Gump told her son, Forrest, "Life's a box of chocolates,

Forrest. You never know what you're gonna get." All truth is parallel. Therefore, "Kids are like a box of chocolates; you never know what you're gonna get." What do I mean by this?

Some children are born with a peaceful temperament, while others seem to rant and rave day and night. Some children are shy, while others are outgoing. Children can be introspective, extroverted, humorous, aggressive or fearful. Some possess a spirited nature that can test the patience and skill of most parents.

It is possible that behavior may be a spirit or it may be inspired by the human spirit (personality). Discernment of spirits, one of the gifts of the Spirit, must be in operation to determine if any demons are involved:

1 Corinthians 12:6-7 and 10-11

And there are diversities of operations, but it is the same God which worketh all in all. But the manifestation of the Spirit is given to every man to profit withal ... . To another the working of miracles; to another prophecy; to another discerning of spirits;

to another divers kinds of tongues; to another the interpretation of tongues: but all these worketh that one and the selfsame Spirit, dividing to every man severally as he will.

Children are curious, adventurous and persistent and can be "a handful" to raise. These traits, however, are incredibly useful for succeeding in today's competitive world. However, there is a fine line between traits being influenced by demons and productive traits in the child's nature. Discerning will help you to identify the source—demonic or natural.

It is possible for demons to enter a child before he accepts Jesus, then remain dormant or hidden in that child's life until sometime later in life, when some opportunity presents itself for that spirit to manifest itself. This is clearly seen in the story of the boy with the dumb spirit brought to Jesus.

The man who brought the child identified him as his son, but there is no indication about his age. The Greek word *son* just meant *child*. The fact that his father brought him to Jesus may indicate, at the very least, that this child had not yet reached the age of accountability. Is it possible for a young, innocent child to be demon possessed? Clearly it is. Children are vulnerable to demon possession.

Whatever the age of the son, what is clear is that an evil spirit was responsible for his condition. Perhaps this son had opened doors in his life to this spirit, or it may well have been brought in through family ties.

As we consider further this passage, it is important that we clear up what legal grounds can give Satan access to our children:

Mark 9:20-22

> *And they brought him* [the child] *unto him* [Jesus]*: and when he saw him, straightway the spirit tare him; and he fell on the ground, and wallowed foaming. And he asked his father, how long is it ago since this came unto him? And he said, Of a child. And ofttimes it hath cast him into the fire, and into the waters, to destroy him: but if thou canst do anything, have compassion on us, and help us.*

It is important to clarify here that not every tantrum a two-year-old throws is a demon-inspired outburst.

Often, medicine or therapy can help a child who is displaying symptoms of uncontrollable behavior, when demonic possession is not suspected. However, in cases where a spiritual problem *is* definitely the root cause, spiritual remedies are necessary, for no medicine will help.

Since the passage does not give the exact age of the possessed child, it is difficult to draw any exact conclusions from it—except to reveal that even children can come under the influence of Satan. God, however, has power to deliver children, as well as adults.

Not yet being at the age of accountability does not prevent a young child from becoming involved in evil things. How many children under the age of twelve are even now in juvenile correction centers? And some of them are downright evil, possibly even possessed. The reality, however, is this: in the face of the influence of Satan on a child, through fervent prayer and an act of deliverance, any child can be set free.

Since demon spirits are able to gain entrance to children, it is obvious that there should be deliverance for them. Demons can be called out of children in the same way they are called out of adults. Casting out demons is one of the signs that is to follow every believer (see Mark 16:17).

Typically, children are quite easily delivered. Since the spirits have not been there a long time, they are not as deeply embedded in the flesh as they might be in someone later on in life. There are exceptions to this, as in the cases of children who have been exposed to demonic attack through severe circumstances. The manifestations of the demons can be quite dramatic, even in children. [2]

Some common spirits found in young children of Christian parents are:

- A tormenting spirit. Such a spirit can enter when parents disagree as to how to properly discipline the child.
- Rebelliousness and unmanageability are an indication of spirits operating in a child.
- When a child is afraid every night and wants to make sure all the doors are locked, this can indicate the presence of demons.
- When children get up at night to get a drink or

2. Hammond, Frank. *Pigs in the Parlor: A handbook for Deliverance from Demons and Spiritual Oppression.* (Kindle Locations 1125-1130). Impact Christian Books. Kindle Edition.

go to the bathroom and are afraid, this might indicate a spirit of fear in their body.

- When a child makes statements such as: "I don't like what you are saying to me, Shut up!" or "You don't love me!" this might indicate a spirit of rejection. Rejection spirits shut children off from loving relationships and make them think that no one loves them. Often such children even think that God doesn't love them.
- If the child says, "I hate you," this may indicate a demon of hate. "I want a weapon to hurt (or kill) you," may indicate a demon of murder and/or a spirit of violence.
- If a child stands up, throws his shoulders back, put his hands on his hips and states, "Nobody EVER tells me what to do!" this may indicate the presence of a spirit of defiance.
- "I do only what I want to do" may indicate the presence of a self-willed demon.
- "You will never make me do what I don't want to do" may indicate a stubbornness spirit.
- If the child attempts to attack you, raising their hands like claws and lunging for you, with their

eyes protruding, and screaming, this may indicate a spirit of madness.

- If the child becomes violent toward himself, this may indicate a spirit of mental illness, insanity or a spirit of schizophrenia. A spirit of schizophrenia may be identified by observing two opposite personalities being exhibited. One of them is rooted in rejection and self-pity, and the other is rooted in rebellion and bitterness. Neither one of these personalities is the real person. You can release and loose the real person to be what Jesus wants them to be in the name of Jesus.

THE NEEDED DELIVERANCE METHOD

When working with children, care must be given to handle their deliverance in such a way as not to further traumatize them.

It is not the loudness of a command that moves the demon, but the authority of the name of Jesus and the blood of Jesus. The command to come out and torment that person no longer can be given with calmness and matter-of-factness, so that the child will scarcely realize what is taking place.

After deliverance, a child is covered by the blood of Jesus through the parent's relationship to Him. Just as the father, in the days of Moses, sprinkled blood on the doorposts of his house for the protection of the entire family, so a child today must be under the covering of the blood.

If your child is not influenced by evil spirits, you can manage their behavior. Provide structure for your child to help him learn to live within limits. Then use methods of discipline to enforce the limits of the situation.

Avoid discipline that is too harsh, but do not fail to offer discipline as needed. Understand that effective discipline includes empathy and problem-solving.

Lastly, teach your child to problem solve for himself. Help him to identify alternative solutions and anticipate consequences. Teach him to identify his feelings, as well as his desires. Use effective communication skills to provide opportunities for teaching him empathy for others. This will help him learn to resolve conflicts cooperatively.

The Scriptures teach:

Ephesians 5:15

See then that ye walk circumspectly, not as fools, but as wise.

According to *The KJV Dictionary,* this word *circumspectly* means: "cautiously; with watchfulness every way; with attention to guard against surprise or danger."[3] Teaching a child to walk circumspectly arms them with the most productive result of their traits.

HOW CHILDREN ARE AFFECTED BY OUR WORDS

The words or actions of a person in authority carry a lot of clout (power) with a child. A parent has authority over their offspring, and the power of a parent can have a profound effect on his or her children (in either a positive or negative way). There is power in the words we speak over our children lives.

A child's life can change forever simply by what a parent speaks over them. Words spoken by a parent can even affect future generations. What is spoken *to* them, *about* them or *at* them can change the trajectory of their life. We can verify this by looking at what Noah did:

3, https://av1611.com/kjbp/kjv-dictionary/circumspectly.html

Genesis 9:20–27, GW

Noah, a farmer, was the first person to plant a vineyard. He drank some wine, got drunk, and lay naked inside his tent. Ham, father of Canaan, saw his father naked. So he went outside and told his two brothers.

Shem and Japheth took a blanket and laid it over their shoulders. Then they walked in backwards and covered their father's naked body. They turned their faces away so that they didn't see their father naked.

When Noah sobered up, he found out what his youngest son had done to him. So he said, "Canaan is cursed!

He will be the lowest slave to his brothers.

Praise the LORD, the God of Shem!

Canaan will be his slave.

May God expand the territory of Japheth.

May he live in the tents of Shem.

Canaan will be his slave."

Noah learned from his younger sons, Shem and Japheth, that Ham had disrespected him, and therefore he spoke against the family of Ham, his oldest son. Note that it was Ham who saw his father naked, but it was his son upon whom the curse was pronounced.

Noah could have cursed Ham because of his actions toward his father. It was Ham who opened the door and gave place to the devil. Unfortunately, it wasn't Ham who suffered because of it but the next generation instead.

We have often heard it said, "What God has blessed, no man can curse." That only applies if there is nothing giving opportunity for Satan to legally enter.

Whether what Noah did was a result of frustration, anger or the effects of the alcohol, it is not clear. But what is clear is that he did not take his frustration out on the guilty party. Instead, for some reason, he directed his rage at his innocent grandson, Canaan, the son of Ham.

Amazingly, Canaan had nothing to do with this entire matter. Still, Noah prophesied (spoke) against Canaan, and a powerful curse was introduced and transferred to future generations. As a result, whole nations of people are still suffering and/or subject to bondage today. Although neither Canaan nor his future generations deserved to be cursed, they were.

In the same way, parents today can curse future generations, or a generation before may have been cursed long ago, and it is still manifesting itself in their children's children.

Again, in the first of the Ten Commandments, we see how the sins of previous generations can affect future generations:

Exodus 20:3-6, GW

> *Never have any other god. Never make your own carved idols or statues that represent any creature in the sky, on the earth, or in the water. Never worship them or serve them, because I, the* Lord *your God, am a God who does not tolerate rivals. I punish children for their parents' sins to the third and fourth generation of those who hate me. But I show mercy to thousands of generations of those who love me and obey my commandments.*

Be careful not to curse your children and grandchildren. And if some inherited curse is upon them, help them to be free of it.

CHAPTER 3

UNDERSTANDING STRONGHOLDS

2 Corinthians 10:4

(For the weapons of our warfare are not carnal, but mighty through God to the pulling down of strong holds.)

Where do strongholds come from? One of the primary weapons the enemy uses against the believer is deception. Deception is a lie appearing to be truth. Strongholds are built upon deception. These deceptions can come from many sources, such as our environment, those around us, our parents or even demon spirits.

Many people are living a defeated life because of what they choose to believe or hold on to. We must pull down those strongholds of deception.

The fact that we must pull down strongholds indicates that there is a fortified wall placed around ideas to protect a thought that must be pulled down. The Greek word translated *stronghold* denotes "to fortify through the idea of holding safely, such as a castle." To *fortify* means "to strengthen a place with defensive walls, to protect it against attack." A *fortress* is "a structure or place from which one can resist attacks." *Fortress* is the Greek word for *stronghold.*

Medieval cities were fortified against attacks by high walls. Volunteers may fortify a levee against flooding by placing sandbags to reinforce it. Foods can be fortified by adding vitamins to them. By adopting good exercise habits, you can fortify your body against illness. Fortifying what we believe, whether it is true or false, uses the same principle. Ultimately a stronghold is a wall of protection placed around what we believe, to strengthen what we believe to be true.

Today a stronghold is a metaphor that represent things that are based only on human confidence or pride, as opposed to those that rely on God's input and guidance. [4] Strongholds are walls or fortresses around beliefs and emotions to protect us from further pain. An important part of healing and transforming deep wounds requires divinely pulling down any existing strongholds.

The word *strongholds* is found only once in the New Testament. There it was used metaphorically, by Paul, in a description of the Christian's spiritual battle:

2 Corinthians 10:3-4, NASB

For though we walk in the flesh, we do not war according to the flesh, for the weapons of our warfare are not of the flesh, but divinely powerful for the destruction of fortresses [strongholds].

Our battle is not fought according to the way this world fights. We are not concerned with earthly strategy. Our weapons are not physical, because our fight is spiritual. We cannot depend on weapons of a physical nature, for our power comes from God alone. His plan is to demolish spiritual strongholds in our lives.

4. www.qa.answers.com/Q/What_is_the_Biblical_defination_of_a_stronghold

The enemy carefully erects a fortified wall, to resist the Truth, to prevent God's plan from mastering your life. His walls are in the form of human reasoning, learned and acquired behavior patterns and logic that tends to protect what the enemy wants you to believe. With passionate defenses, you protect and reinforce what you believe. In this way, the enemy can firmly entrench himself in a belief system, making it into a stronghold that guards against and resists Truth.

Strongholds formed in our minds are typically known as "imaginations." An imagination can create a false concept that you believe to be true. In reality, it is not true. The Bible speaks clearly about such imaginations, and shows us how they can be torn down:

2 Corinthians 10:5

Casting down imaginations, and every high thing that exalteth itself against the knowledge of God, and bringing into captivity every thought to the obedience of Christ.

"*Casting down* **imaginations** *and every* **high thing** ... ." The *imaginations* and *high things* form the stronghold, and so these are the operative words. The Greek word translated *imaginations* is *log-is-mos'*; from G3049 and denotes, "a reckoning, computation, i.e. reasoning that is hostile to the Christian faith and conscience." *Imagination* also means "a judgment or decision."

High thing is from the Greek G5313 *hoop'-so-mah*; from G5312 and denotes "an elevated place or thing, i.e. (abstractly) attitude, or (by implication) a barrier (figuratively): height."

Paul wrote to the Roman believers:

Romans 2:14-15

For when the Gentiles, which have not the law, do by nature the things contained in the law, these, having not the law, are a law unto themselves: which shew the work of the law written in their hearts, their conscience also bearing witness, and their thoughts the mean while accusing or else excusing one another.

The conscience and thoughts have a way of protecting what you believe to be true. Your truth may be in line with the Word of God, or it may actually be in opposition to the Word of God. If we are to live in victory, it is very important that we have right thinking. Our thoughts are very powerful, as they shape our behavior, and our behavior shapes our lives. The only effective defensive weapon against the lies of the enemy is the Word of God. When the Word is applied to the protective walls the enemy has carefully built up over time, his false protection is dissolved.

Be free though the truth of God's Word!

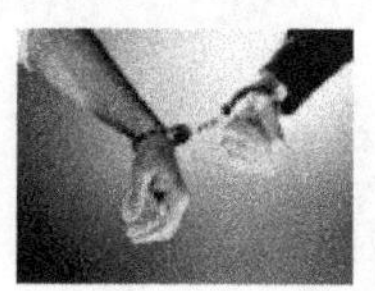

CHAPTER 4

AWAKENED ANCESTRAL SPIRITS

Matthew 18:21-22, GW

Then Peter came to Jesus and asked him, "Lord, how often do I have to forgive a believer who wrongs me? Seven times?"

Jesus answered him, "I tell you, not just seven times, but seventy times seven."

I mentioned earlier that sometimes a generational curse can remain latent in our lives for years and then suddenly surface. What might awaken ancestral spirits in your life? Unforgiveness is a great way to awaken ancestral spirits. Bitterness or unforgiveness in your heart is a sure way of bringing hidden spirits to the forefront.

Unforgiveness gives legal grounds for the enemy to plague your life. It gives the enemy full access to erect strongholds in your mind.

It would be worth our while to see more of this important passage from Matthew 18:

Matthew 18:21-34, GW

Then Peter came to Jesus and asked him, "Lord, how often do I have to forgive a believer who wrongs me? Seven times?"
Jesus answered him, "I tell you, not just seven times, but seventy times seven.
"That is why the kingdom of heaven is like a king who wanted to settle accounts with his servants. When he began to do this, a servant who owed him millions of dollars was brought to him. Because he could not pay off the debt, the master ordered him, his wife, his children, and all that he had to be sold to pay off the account. Then the servant fell at his master's feet and said, 'Be patient with me, and I will repay everything!'

"The master felt sorry for his servant, freed him, and canceled his debt. But when that servant went away, he found a servant who owed him hundreds of dollars. He grabbed the servant he found and began to choke him. 'Pay what you owe!' he said.

"Then that other servant fell at his feet and begged him, 'Be patient with me, and I will repay you.' But he refused. Instead, he turned away and had that servant put into prison until he would repay what he owed.

"The other servants who worked with him saw what had happened and felt very sad. They told their master the whole story.

"Then his master sent for him and said to him, 'You evil servant! I canceled your entire debt, because you begged me. Shouldn't you have treated the other servant as mercifully as I treated you?'

"His master was so angry that he handed him over to the torturers until he would repay everything that he owed."

From these scriptures, we can see that our actions can give the tormentor legal access to our lives. It is important never to allow your emotions to control your actions.

In this passage of scripture, the man forgiven then refused to extend mercy to a person who owed him something. As a result, he was severely punished for his refusal to forgive as he had been forgiven and release the debt of another as he had been released from his debt.

Again, curses may be canceled and the demons that caused them may remain with a person. Just as other demons don't automatically leave at the time of salvation, neither do demons that have entered in through the actions of your ancestors. The curse may be cast out, but the demon that brought it does not automatically leave. You must treat the curse separate from the spirit that brought the curse. Deal decisively with awakened ancestral spirits.

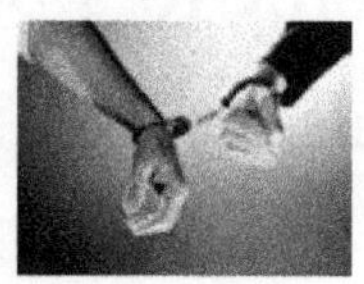

CHAPTER 5

SOME BASIC STEPS OF DELIVERANCE

Ephesians 4:27

Neither give place to the devil.

In all of this, it is important to know a few basic steps of deliverance.

Confess: Confess any sin. Sin gives Satan a legal right to occupy a place in your life.

Repent: Repentance is a determined turning away from sin and Satan. You must hate all evil in your life and no longer agree with sin and Satan. Ezekiel declared:

Ezekiel 20:43

And there shall ye remember your ways, and all your doings, wherein ye have been defiled; and ye shall lothe yourselves in your own sight for all your evils that ye have committed.

Any sin not confessed or repented of will give a demon a legal right to remain.

David recognized his sin before God:

Psalm 32:5

I acknowledged my sin unto thee, and mine iniquity have I not hid. I said, I will confess my transgressions unto the LORD; and thou forgavest the iniquity of my sin. Selah.

Psalm 139:23-24

Search me, O God, and know my heart: try me, and know my thoughts: and see if there be any wicked way in me, and lead me in the way everlasting.

Renounce the Curse: Renunciation is a clean break with Satan and all his works. An example is found in Acts 19:

Acts 19:18-19

And many that believed came, and confessed, and shewed their deeds. Many of them also which used curious arts brought their books together, and burned them before all men: and they counted the price of them, and found it fifty thousand pieces of silver.

Demonstrate Your Determination: Give evidence that you have truly turned from you sin. For example, if you have repented of lust, you may need to destroy some pornographic materials. If you have repented of religious error, you may need to completely renounce it by destroying all the literature or other items associated with that error.

Do Warfare: Prayer and warfare are two separate and distinct activities. Prayer is toward God and warfare is toward the enemy. Our warfare against demon powers is not fleshly but spiritual (see Ephesians 6:10-12 and 2 Corinthians 10:3-5).

Use Your Weapons: These are the weapons of submission to God, the blood of Jesus Christ, the Word of

God and your testimony as a believer (see James 4:7, Ephesians 6:17 and Revelation 12:11).

Identify the Spirits: Address the offending spirits directly and by name in a commanding voice. Then, in faith, command them to go in the name of Jesus.

Be Determined: Enter this battle with determination and assurance of victory. Christ cannot fail! He is our Deliverer!

Consider God's promises:

Mark 16:17

And these signs shall follow them that believe; In my name shall they cast out devils.

Luke 10:19

Behold, I give unto you power to tread on serpents and scorpions, and over all the power of the enemy: and nothing shall by any means hurt you.

Psalm 18:2

The LORD is my rock, and my fortress, and my deliverer.

Believing God's promises, act on them, claiming your freedom from all ancestral curses and/or their accompanying demons.

CHAPTER 6

THE IMPORTANCE OF CONFESSION FOR YOUR SOUL

Romans 4:17

(As it is written, I have made thee a father of many nations,) before him whom he believed, even God, who quickeneth the dead, and calleth those things which be not as though they were.

There is power in our verbal confessions, and they help us to realize that we are set free. By making confessions, we let the enemy know that he's in trouble! Confessing what is rightfully ours is an amazing privilege God has granted us so that we may create our destiny. Your words keep you in alignment with God's perfect will.

As noted, generational curses have been broken in Jesus' name by His finished work on the cross, but you can verbally confess what you know God has done and will do *for* you and *with* you in the coming days. It is always an encouragement to confess those things which are not as though they were.

Paul wrote the Corinthians believers:

1 Corinthians 1:26-28

For ye see your calling, brethren, how that not many wise men after the flesh, not many mighty, not many noble, are called: but God hath chosen the foolish things of the world to confound the wise; and God hath chosen the weak things of the world to confound the things which are mighty; and base things of the world, and things which are despised, hath God chosen, yea, and things which are not, to bring to nought things that are.

God has chosen this method to initiate change in our lives. But some don't know that this scripture is even in the Bible, even when they have read it many times. God chose this method of using things that are not manifest (things that you cannot see with the natural eye) to bring to nought the things that are manifest.

Nought means "zero" and *to bring to nought* means "to reduce to nothing." With your words, you can reduce to nothing things that are.

The Greek word for *naught* G2673 denotes "to render idle, unemployed, inactivate, inoperative; to cause a person or thing to have no further efficiency; to deprive of force, power to cause to cease, put an end to, do away with, annul, abolish; to cease, to pass away, be done away; to be severed from, separated from, discharged from, loosed from; to terminate all intercourse with one." [5] That's powerful, and you and I can do it with our words of confession.

Another important passage we should consider is 2 Corinthians 4:

2 Corinthians 4:13 and 17-18

We having the same spirit of faith, according as it

5. https://www.blueletterbible.org/lang/lexicon/lexicon.cfm?t=nasb&strongs=g 2673

is written, I believed, and therefore have I spoken; we also believe, and therefore speak.

For our light affliction, which is but for a moment, worketh for us a far more exceeding and eternal weight of glory; while we look not at the things which are seen, but at the things which are not seen: for the things which are seen are temporal; but the things which are not seen are eternal.

Confession is a biblical principle that God chose to use for His glory and our blessing. He chose to use things that are not manifest—spiritual forces that you cannot see, feel, taste, smell or hear—to bring to nought the things that are manifest. He chose this method to reduce to nought those things that do not agree with His Word.

If you have a problem and you can see it, then it's in the natural realm. As long as you can see it, you can use your faith and the Word of God to change it. Make your declaration today.

The unseen realm is a powerful realm, one governed by God's eternal principles. God chooses to call things that are *not* manifest as though they *were* manifest. And you, too, can call for eternal forces that put to nought things that are seen. You can call into manifestation the things that are not, and they will replace what is now manifest.

Here is an important thought to consider: There is a great difference between calling things that are not as though they were and calling things that are as though they were not. God does not mean for us to deny what exists. You don't call things that *are* as though they *are not*. God's method is to call things that *are not* manifest as though they *were* manifest.

Here's a great sample confession prayer you can use in this regard:

> **In the name of Jesus, I confess the sins and iniquities of my parents (name specific sins if they are known), grandparents (name specific sins if they are known), and all other ancestors. I declare that by the blood of Jesus, these sins have been forgiven, and Satan and his demons can no longer use these sins as legal grounds in my life!**

In the name of Jesus and by the power of His blood, I now declare that all generational curses have been renounced, broken and severed, and that I am no longer under their bondage!
In the name of Jesus, I declare myself and my future generations loosed from any and all bondages passed down to me from my ancestors.

AMEN!

CHAPTER 7

WIDE PORTALS AND OPENED DOORS

Psalm 24:7, KJ21

Lift your heads, O ye gates!
And be lifted up, ye everlasting doors!
And the King of glory shall come in.

One of the marvelous mysteries of God is the existence of portals—doors and passageways leading to and from the heavenly realms. Throughout the Scriptures, as in Psalm 24:7, we see the existence of such doorways or portals:

Psalm 78:23

Though he had commanded the clouds from above and opened the doors of heaven.

Proverbs 8:34, GW

Blessed is the person who listens to me, watches at my door day after day, and waits by my doorposts.

John 1:51, NKJV

Most assuredly, I say to you, hereafter you shall see heaven open, and the angels of God ascending and descending upon the Son of Man.

Revelation 4:1-2, NKJV

After these things I looked, and behold, a door standing open in heaven. And the first voice which I heard was like a trumpet speaking with me, saying, "Come up here, and I will show you things which must take place after this." Immediately, I was in the Spirit.

In Genesis 28, the Bible calls a portal *"the gate of heaven"*:

Genesis 28:12-13 and 15-17

And he dreamed, and behold a ladder set up on the earth, and the top of it reached to heaven: and behold the angels of God ascending and descending on it. And, behold, the Lord stood above it, and said, I am the Lord God of Abraham thy father, and the God of Isaac. ...

And, behold, I am with thee, and will keep thee in all places whither thou goest, and will bring thee again into this land; for I will not leave thee, until I have done that which I have spoken to thee of. And Jacob awaked out of his sleep, and he said, Surely the Lord is in this place; and I knew it not. And he was afraid, and said, How dreadful is this place! this is none other but the house of God, and this is the gate of heaven.

Jacob's ladder, in Genesis 28:12, speaks of a portal where the angels of God were ascending and descending through the passageway between Earth and Heaven. A heavenly portal is a spherical opening of light that offers divine protection by which angels and heavenly beings can come and go, without demonic interference. God has designed portals to begin in the third Heaven, travel through the second Heaven and open upon the Earth.

In simple terms, a spirit portal is a doorway in the physical world that allows free access to and from the spirit world. The existence of a portal can rely on a vortex of energy to sustain it. This is an area of mass energy in high concentration, usually originating from magnetic, spiritual or sometimes unknown sources that create powerful eddies that manifest a spiral of energy which can be positive or negative in nature. [6]

John also spoke about a portal where the angels of God ascended and descended upon Jesus, the Son of Man (see John 1:51). He called this portal an open heaven.

So, an open heaven is an open portal in the third Heaven where the angels of God can ascend and descend without delay or interference from satanic forces in the second Heaven.

THE THREE HEAVENS

Let's take a minute to understand the three heavens:

---

6. http://supernaturalmagazine.com/articles/spirit-portals-and-energy-vortexes

The First Heaven is the firmament, Earth's atmosphere, which is the immediate sky. In the first heaven, the *"fowls of the heaven"* (Genesis 2:19, 7:3 and 23 and Psalm 8:8) or *"the eagles of heaven"* (Lamentations 4:19) fly. Simply stated, the first heaven is the atmosphere that surrounds our Earth.

The Second Heaven is outer space, the starry heavens (see Deuteronomy 17:3, Jeremiah 8:2 and Matthew 24:29). The second heaven is the heavens where the sun, moon and stars are fixed in orbit. The stars are seemingly endless, and the distance between all of them is staggering. No wonder the Bible states, in Psalm 19:1 (NKJV), *"The heavens declare the glory of God; and the firmament shows His handiwork."* In ancient times, people were in awe of the starry expanse. Today, we know how immense it really is.

The Third Heaven is where God and the holy angels (and creatures) and the spirits of just men dwell. It is called *"The heaven of heavens" or "highest heaven"* (Deuteronomy 10:14, 1 Kings 8:27, Psalm 115:16,

148:4 and 1 Kings 8:27). This Heaven is the dwelling-place of God to which Paul was taken and whose wonders he was permitted to behold. Simply stated, the third Heaven is the region where God dwells.

All truth is parallel. Therefore, if God's angels have access to heavenly portals, or doors, of access, so do Satan and his hordes of evil spirit. He gains this access when sin opens a portal to him.

Satan was originally one of God's holy angels, but he rebelled against God and was cast out of Heaven. In Luke 10, Jesus addressed the seventy believers who returned after being sent out to proclaim His Good News. Before He gave them power, Jesus informed them that Satan, who had once occupied a place in Heaven, no longer resided there. He had been cast out:

Luke 10:17-19

And the seventy returned again with joy, saying, Lord, even the devils are subject unto us through thy name. And he said unto them, I beheld Satan as lightning fall from heaven. Behold, I give unto you power to tread on serpents and scorpions, and over all the power of the enemy: and nothing shall by any means hurt you.

That was only the first stage of Satan's judgment. He will eventually be bound in the abyss for a thousand years:

Revelation 20:1-3

And I saw an angel come down from heaven, having the key of the bottomless pit and a great chain in his hand. And he laid hold on the dragon, that old serpent, which is the Devil, and Satan, and bound him a thousand years, and cast him into the bottomless pit, and shut him up, and set a seal upon him, that he should deceive the nations no more, till the thousand years should be fulfilled: and after that he must be loosed a little season.

Later, the ultimate defeat of Satan will come when he is cast into the Lake of Fire for eternity:

Revelation 20:10

And the devil that deceived them was cast into the

lake of fire and brimstone, where the beast and the false prophet are, and shall be tormented day and night for ever and ever.

Until his final judgment in complete, however, Satan remains *"the prince of this world"*:

John 14:30

Hereafter I will not talk much with you: for the prince of this world cometh, and hath nothing in me.

God has given Satan restricted access to the heavenly realms. The phrase *"god of this world"* (or *"god of this age"*) indicates that Satan is the major influence on the ideals, opinions, goals, hopes and views of most people today. His influence also includes the world's values, education and business. The thoughts, ideas, theories and false religions of the world are under his control and are birthed through his lies and deceptions.

Satan is also called the *"prince of the power of the air"*:

Ephesians 2:2

Wherein in time past ye walked according to the course of this world, according to the prince of the power of the air, the spirit that now worketh in the children of disobedience.

Why is Satan termed *"the prince of the power of the air"*? Because the air is the region where malicious spirits live, and those spirits are under the direction and influence of Satan, their overlord. These spirits can influence people because they reside in the air around us. When sin is present, a portal is opened which allows the spirit free legal access, not only to influence us, but also to overreach and try to meddle in the life of a believer.

Satan is the *"ruler of this world"* (John 12:31). These titles and many more signify his capabilities. To say, for example, that Satan is *"the prince of the power of the air"* is to signify that in some way he rules over this world and the people in it.

However, Satan does not rule the world completely. God is still sovereign. But God, in His infinite wisdom, has allowed Satan to operate in this world within the boundaries He has set for him.

When the Bible says that Satan has power over the world, we must remember that God has given him domain over unbelievers only. Believers are no longer under the rule of Satan:

Colossians 1:13, NKJV

He has delivered us from the power of darkness and [a]conveyed us into the kingdom of the Son of His love.

If a portal exists for Satan to enter our lives, we need to become aware of that portal, and we need to confront it and close it. For too long the enemy has had portals operating in certain cities and nations, and through the activity of the people he influences there, he can bring deception and destruction. Unfortunately, the Church has ignored these possibilities.

When we go into an area to start a church or to have some special meetings, we need to be aware that such portals exist and will be operating. We need to come together in unity and close these portals as the Lord reveals them.

This is not something to be taken lightly. We must rise up in the power and authority of Jesus and, through a prayer of agreement, shut any existing evil portals.

Unity of purpose is the key to victory in this regard:

Psalm 133:1-3

Behold, how good and how pleasant it is for brethren to dwell together in unity! It is like the precious ointment upon the head, that ran down upon the beard, even Aaron's beard: that went down to the skirts of his garments; as the dew of Hermon, and as the dew that descended upon the mountains of Zion: for there the LORD commanded the blessing, even life for evermore.

And, just as we have the authority and power in unity to close evil portals, we also have the authority and power in unity to open godly portals into the third Heaven. Revivals come where there is an open heaven.

The windows of Heaven are mentioned in Malachi:

Malachi 3:10

Bring ye all the tithes into the storehouse, that there may be meat in mine house, and prove me now herewith, saith the LORD of hosts, if I will not open you the windows of heaven, and pour you out a blessing, that there shall not be room enough to receive it.

A door in Heaven is mentioned in Revelation 4, as it relates to a throne there:

Revelation 4:1

After this I looked, and, behold, a door was opened in heaven: and the first voice which I heard was as it were of a trumpet talking with me; which said, Come up hither, and I will shew thee things which must be hereafter.

The *"door"* in Revelation suggests God's invitation for us to have access to His heavenly realm. For His children, the Lord wants to open the portals of

Heaven and release an unparalleled visitation of heavenly hosts.

JACOB DISCOVERED A HEAVENLY PORTAL

Jacob spent the night in a place where his forefather Abraham had *"called upon the name of the Lord"* (Genesis 12:8). As Jacob laid his head upon a stone, a portal opened, and he saw a vision of the ladder, with angels ascending and descending on it.

When he awoke from sleep, Jacob said:

Genesis 28:16-17

Surely the Lord is in this place; and I knew it not. And he was afraid, and said, How dreadful is this place! this is none other but the house of God, and this is the gate of heaven.

Enthusiastic to mark the experience and the specific location where he had encountered the stairway to Heaven, Jacob erected a monument and named the place Bethel or "dwelling place of God." Several times after this, the Lord told

Jacob to return to Bethel, where He would speak to him. This indicates that the place you have an experience with God may become the geographic location of a spiritual portal where God can connect with you.

The point is that you and I must become attuned to the existence of spiritual portals—for good or for bad.

CHAPTER 8

RECOGNIZING THE SIGNS OF A STRONGHOLD

2 Corinthians 10:4

(For the weapons of our warfare are not carnal, but mighty through God to the pulling down of strong holds.)

The Greek word for *stronghold* is actually a military term, and it means "fortress." In ancient times, a soldier would erect a fortress in an area in which the enemy was known to roam. That is what it means when we speak of Satan's *stronghold* in the life of a person. Satan becomes entrenched in an area of a person's life where there is a character flaw, an emotional or psychological tendency to selfish attitudes and/or behaviors.

Satan's strongholds often take advantage of physical needs or weaknesses. For example, physical appetites for food and physical appetites for sex open doors to him. Any physical indulgence, when it is not yielded to God, creates an open portal for Satan to come in and build a stronghold.

A stronghold is a pattern of thinking that keeps us from fully connecting with God. These are areas where our weakness has flourished, and bad habits are born. Some strongholds are obvious. A terrible temper would be a stronghold of anger. Other strongholds are subtler or mask themselves as being productive habits. A person who works hard could be suffering from a stronghold of greed. They may have unintentionally let the desire for money consume their life and distract them from both meaningful human relationships and their relationship with God. Their work ethic, that appears to be a positive trait, may, instead, be a spiritual stronghold that takes their heart and focus away from God.

Other strongholds may be emotional or psychological. Whether physical, emotional, psychological or spiritual in origin, strongholds are areas of bondage to Satan. He has free reign to strengthen and spread his control over a given individual who has fallen prey to this trick of his.

Satan uses many human weaknesses, emotions and tendencies to establish strongholds. Some of the signs of strongholds are compulsions, obsessions, fears, lusts, jealousies, violent tempers and uncontrolled appetites of all kinds. These are only a few of the signs that a stronghold is either being built or has been firmly established in a life.

In an article "Subtle Signs You Need to Start Breaking Strongholds" by Stephanie Hertzenberg, she lists six signs that she observed as strongholds. I have adapted her list to help our understanding:

LOW SELF-ESTEEM

There are many causes for low self-esteem. One common cause is perfectionism. You feel that because you make mistakes, you are somehow worth less as a person. This, of course, is not true. No human can be perfect. We are, by our very nature, fallible.

Another cause of low self-esteem could be rooted in vanity. If you think you are fat and are ashamed of your body, your self-esteem will suffer. The same is true if you look in the mirror and wish that your teeth were straighter or your legs longer.

Your physical appearance, of course, is not what matters in God's eyes. Accepting your appearance—imperfections and all—can be difficult due to our constant exposure to what is marketed as the "right" look. The media is filled with Photoshopped images of both men and women, and half the commercials on TV seem to be for various weight-loss systems. Remind yourself that it is not the appearance of your flesh that matters, but the purity of your heart.

KEEPING YOUR PASSIONS OR TALENTS TO YOURSELF

You think that you are protecting yourself from rejection or harm. Stop holding yourself back. God gave you the gifts you possess for a reason. You should make use of them. Show off your talent. Teach others to embrace their gifts. Trusting someone with something you have worked hard on is not always easy, but if you never show anyone what you've done, the doubts will continue to plague you. You may get a positive response that boosts your confidence. You may also get constructive criticism that allows you to continue honing the gifts you were given.

IMPATIENCE

We all have moments when we become impatient. We have all been frustrated by the slow-moving car that insists on sitting in the passing lane, when we are running late for work. We have all been there when the man in front of us at the grocery store can't decide if he really wants to keep the bananas he thought were on sale. We stand there and tap our toes or check our watches, ready to be somewhere else.

We've all experienced those moments. Occasionally being impatient is not a problem. It is when you are always impatient that you need to start breaking strongholds.

Impatience is a twisted combination of anger and pride. We feel that where we are going or what we are doing is more important than what anyone else is doing. We are then angry when we are delayed by what we see as less important issues. Impatience blinds us to other people's lives and turns our focus inward. We see only our own wants and needs and become selfish.

DEFENSIVENESS

If you find yourself taking things personally, it might be time to start breaking strongholds. Defensiveness is a nasty mix of anger and insecurity. Someone accidentally steps on your insecurity, and you feel personally attacked. You get angry and lash out with spiteful words. You push away friends and loved ones, convinced that they are trying to hurt you or get under your skin. This is not a healthy response or the sort of response God would want.

Defensiveness often goes hand in hand with the inability to accept criticism gracefully. You might ignore the critique completely, pridefully assuming you know better. You might also do the opposite and take the correction of a mistake to mean that you are incapable and lose all motivation.

Neither of these reactions is a healthy one or one favorable to keeping our hearts turned toward God. No human being is perfect. We all make mistakes and we all have room for improvement. When you become overly defensive, it is a sign that you have forgotten this truth.

SELF-ISOLATION

This stronghold is almost always caused by fear. You may have been hurt before and fear that you will be hurt again. You may believe that you will be rejected if you try to form another connection with someone. Perhaps you suffered from a betrayal and are suspicious of getting close to someone again.

Regardless of the reason, it is not healthy to isolate yourself. To break this stronghold, you must face your fears. You must try to connect with other people. Pray for strength to overcome your fear of being hurt. Forgive the person who betrayed you, and create a new connection to fill the hole they left behind. Human beings were not meant to be alone. We are social creatures and depend on each other.

There is also the danger that isolating yourself will diminish your empathy toward those who are suffering. If you isolate yourself, you have fewer reasons to care about the world you fear will reject you. You become less sympathetic and less likely to reach out to those who need you.

FEELING HOPELESS

If you find yourself thinking life will never improve or that things will be bad forever, you need to start breaking strongholds. God is all-loving and all-merciful. Challenges and trials are meant to test our faith and teach us lessons we would otherwise not learn. Our struggles are meant to teach us strength, and our suffering is meant to teach us to empathize with others.

When you feel hopeless, remember that there are lessons to be learned in every trial. Look for the lesson you are meant to be learning, and remind yourself that your struggles will not last forever. Instead of obsessing over problems, focus instead on the blessings you *do* have in your life. God leaves blessings in every situation—if you look hard enough for them. Remember, God loves you and is always with you, even in the darkest of times.

Breaking strongholds is never easy, but half the battle is realizing they are there. Subtle indicators are easily blamed on other things in our lives, and the root of the problem is left unaddressed. Once we identify a stronghold, we can break it. Having broken the strongholds in our lives, we can show others how to break strongholds in their lives and, in this way, help spread God's love. [7]

Clearly strongholds can be present in the life of Christians, as well as in unbelievers. In most cases, the individual will recognize that something is out of control, but he or she will almost always say "I've tried to control that, but I can't seem to get on top of it." Most of the time, a person doesn't recognizes that the stronghold is about to destroy their marriage, their family, their career or their reputation.

For the Christian, the presence of a stronghold can have severe consequences. Strongholds cause them to drift away from fellowship with God, cause deep self-doubt and an intense dislike, disgust or even hatred of self. For the unbeliever, the stronghold is Satan's weapon for blocking the voice of the Holy Spirit, as He challenges the sinner to repent.

---

7. http://www.beliefnet.com/wellness/articles/subtle-signs-you-need-to-startbreaking-strongholds.aspx?p=2#Ek2ZPEL4oW3S0doK.99

To break strongholds, we are instructed to use prayers of all kind. Fervent endless prayer, purposeful prayer, when spoken under spiritual authority will penetrate walls that have been erected. Prayer is the warfare, prayer is the engagement, prayer is the assault on the stronghold to bring it down. Be set free by God's power!

CHAPTER 9

PREVENTING SATAN FROM GAINING A FOOTHOLD

Ephesians 4:27

Neither give place to the devil.

Just as important as (or perhaps more important than) being set free from Satan's strongholds is preventing him from ever gaining a foothold in your life. You can convince yourself that a lie is the truth and the truth is a lie. You can be a prisoner of deception and not be aware of it. Your enemy is the devil, and he influences you to erect defensive walls to protect what you have been conditioned in life to believe. Those truths may be justified, or they may be unwarranted.

A quote from Benjamin Franklin is appropriate here: "An ounce of prevention is worth a pound of cure." Taking the initiative to stop something from happening is easier and better than having to try to resolve it later. Ephesians 4:27 is the best advice to consider. Don't even give him a place.

This word *give* in the Greek is *didōmi* (G1325), which denotes "adventure, bestow, bring forth, commit, deliver up, grant, offer, have power, put, set, yield." Do not give the devil an opportunity to use your life to take his journey. Do not allow his journey to become your journey. Do not hand over your character to the opposing forces, allowing them to bring havoc to your life, causing you much pain and frustration.

The word *place* here is the operative word. *Place* in the Greek is *topos*, which denotes "a spot (generally in space, but limited by occupancy)," which means you grant a spot for the devil to occupy. That spot is not available until you provide it. You give the devil power to possess it.

Whereas *chõro* (G5561) is a larger but particular locality, that is, "location (as a position, home, tract, etc.)," this implies that a spiritual position is provided to accommodate the imagination and every high thought that promotes itself against the knowledge of God's truth. It is as if you give a home to the devil to inhabit any area of your life he chooses that this happens.

This indicates that the environment can foster feelings of insecurity that may cause an individual to cover their mind and heart, to protect from being hurt. We are all admonished not to give license nor legal authority to the devil. Nothing could be more important.

The International Standard Version of the Bible renders that thought in this way:

Ephesians 4:27, ISV

and do not give the devil an opportunity to work.

The Tree of Life Version (TLV) renders it as:

nor give the devil a foothold.

The Good News Bible (GNT) renders it:

Don't give the Devil a chance. [8]

When you give the devil a foothold into your life, he makes of it a stronghold. If you give Satan control of one little part of your life, he will soon take over the whole thing.

Satan can use any negative emotion to gain a foothold. Anger, resentment and bitterness are the most common emotions that extend a welcome mat to him. Ephesians 4:26 instructs us in the best way to deal with negative emotions, that is deal with them immediately:

Ephesians 4:26

Be ye angry, and sin not: let not the sun go down upon your wrath.

If negative emotions are left in your heart, you give Satan the opportunity to establish a foothold in your life. Being proactive about dealing with negative emotions will ensure your freedom from such strongholds.

We need to be careful not to compromise what we know is right for some "gray area" pleasure. We need

8. http://rickwarren.org/listen/player

to be clearheaded and attentive that we are not enticed to sin, thereby opening a door for the devil to find a place in our lives.

You and I never have to fall prey to the devil! If we can shut every door, close every window and seal every place in our lives through which the enemy would try to gain admission, we can refuse him admittance. It is sin that creates an entry point.

Another entry point the devil tries to use to enter our lives is through our relationships. If there is an unresolved issue, pain or conflict with a loved one or friend, these conflict points often become entry points through which the devil tries to gain a foothold. Once the enemy can slip in through one of these "cracks" and build an offended place in our minds, then a wall has begun to be constructed that will eventually separate us from the people we need and love the most.

That offense creates a specific, marked-off, geographical location. It carries the idea of a territory, province, region, zone or geographical position. It is from this word *topos* that we get the word for a topographical map. Because *topos* describes a geographical location, this lets us know that the devil is after every region and zone of our lives. His interest in our life is money, health, marriage, relationships, employment, business and ministry. He is so territorial that he wants it all.

To start his operation to conquer all those areas of our lives, Satan must first find an entry point where he can begin his campaign of releasing his destruction in our lives. We often throw open the door to the devil when we do any of the following:

- Refuse to let go of old hurts and wounds.
- Refuse to acknowledge something we ourselves did wrong.
- Refuse to forgive others for something they did to us or to others.
- Refuse to stop judging others for their objections and refuse to admit that we have also been wrong.
- Refuse to say, "I'm sorry" when we're wrong.
- Refuse to lay down our "rights" in a given situation.

If you and I do any of these things, we leave a "marked-off place" through which the devil can enter to accuse others in our minds. We can avoid falling victim to the enemy's tactics. We can merely refuse to give him place, and he will not be able to infiltrate our lives.

We are more than conquerors through Jesus Christ, so we don't have to let the devil run all over us. The Bible boldly declares:

1 John 4:4

Ye are of God, little children, and have overcome them: because greater is he that is in you, than he that is in the world.

We must choose to give the devil no territory whatsoever. We have a choice in this matter. We can choose to give the enemy place in our minds and emotions, or we can choose to walk in the Spirit, not giving Satan a spot to claim. If we choose to give the enemy a place, we will invariably end up doing and saying things we will later regret. Those regretful things are usually what opens the door for the devil to wreak havoc in our relationships. He is looking for any possible entry point.

Once a point has been located through which Satan can secretly slip into people's lives, he begins penetrating their mind and emotions, to drive a wedge between those individuals and the other people in their lives. The enemy's objective is to separate them from each other with his railing, slanderous accusations.

You will know when the accuser has gone to work in your mind because your whole perspective about the person you are upset with will suddenly change. You will become nit-picky, negative and fault-finding about everything. You used to have a high regard for that person, but now you can't see anything good about him or her at all. It is as if you've put on a special set of eyeglasses that are specially designed to reveal all their wicked, ugly, horrid details. Even if you do see something good in them, all the bad you see far outweighs the good.

This is clear evidence that the work of the accuser has found an entry point to penetrate your relationship with that person. He is trying to disrupt what has been, until then, a pleasant and gratifying relationship. Don't allow that conflict, disagreement or disappointment to cause you to pick up a wrong attitude that will ruin your relationship. That's exactly what the enemy wants.

Rather than allow this to happen, stop and tell yourself, "Okay, this isn't as big a deal as I'm making it out to be. The devil is trying to find a place in my mind, to get me to start mentally accusing that person, and I'm not going to let him do that."

Instead of meditating on all the bad points of that person, look in the mirror and consider yourself. How many times have you let other people down? How many mistakes have you made in your relationships? How many times should you have been held accountable when, instead, you were shown unbelievable mercy. Remembering these things about yourself has a way of making you look at an offensive situation with more mercy.

Ask the Holy Spirit to take the criticism out of your heart and to cause the love of God to be in you and to flow out of you toward that other person or group of people. Pray for an opportunity to strengthen your relationship with them so that all the entry places to your life and to that relationship remain sealed. Stop the devil from working his way into the middle of your relationships with people you need and love! Don't give him any space at all. You belong to God.

CHAPTER 10

EXAMINING MORE FULLY THE ROOTS OF ANCESTRAL CURSES

John 12:31

Now is the judgment of this world: now shall the prince of this world be cast out.

John 14:30

Hereafter I will not talk much with you: for the prince of this world cometh, and hath nothing in me.

John 16:11

Of judgment, because the prince of this world is judged.

As we have determined, curses come from the prince of this world and his cohorts located in the second heaven. As a prophetic people, it is important for us to insure that our revelations come from the third Heaven where God resides. Revelations that originate in the second heaven are from Satan, and revelations that originate from the third Heaven are from God. Prophets must learn to distinguish between "second-heaven revelations" (from the devil) and "third-Heaven revelations" (from God).

There is a hierarchy of demonic power, with the first-heaven (earth-bound) demons being of lesser authority and power than the second-heaven demons.

According to Ephesians 6:12, demons are the spiritual force of evil in the heavenly realms:

Ephesians 6:12

For we wrestle not against flesh and blood, but against principalities, against powers, against the rulers of the darkness of this world, against spiritual wickedness in high places.

So ancestral curses come from the prince of this world and his cohorts located in second heaven. Curses are not sent; they are brought by a demon. Listed here are a few ruling spirits that bring curses that may affect your life:

- **A SPIRIT OF POSSESSIVENESS** is assigned to bring, greed, jealousy, laziness, gambling, stinginess, hoarding, stealing, poverty and indebtedness.
- **A SPIRIT OF FEAR** is assigned to bring fear of failure, fear of man, fear of evil, fear of the dark, fear of closed places, fear of heights, fear of losing your salvation, fear of the unknown, panic attacks and anxiety.
- **A SPIRIT OF LUST** is assigned to bring fornication, adultery, pornography, masturbation, homosexuality, incest, sexual abuse of others and rape.
- **A SPIRIT OF ESCAPE** is assigned to bring substance addictions to illegal drugs, prescribed medications, alcohol, tobacco and caffeine.
- **A SPIRIT OF GLUTTONY** is assigned to bring food issues, such as overeating, bulimia and anorexia.

- A **SPIRIT OF ANGER** is assigned to bring unforgiveness, bitterness, hatred, rage, violence, aggressiveness toward others, revenge and murder.
- A **SPIRIT OF REBELLION** is assigned to bring rebellion toward God and authority, stubbornness, pride, idolatry, disobedience and lawlessness.
- A **SPIRIT OF THE OCCULT** is assigned to bring occult involvement such as witchcraft, satanism, consulting a psychic, palm reading or fortune telling, witching for water, using a Ouija board, horoscopes, pendulum, séances and hypnotism.
- A **CRITICAL SPIRIT** is assigned to cause being critical of others, harboring judgmentalism, belittling others, joking at the expense of others, self-righteousness, coldness, general rejection of others, witchcraft, arrogance and a controlling attitude.
- A **SPIRIT OF SLANDER** is assigned to bring an uncontrolled tongue, lying, slander, cursing, swearing, exaggeration, denial, foul mouth and gossip.
- A **SPIRIT OF BREACH** is assigned to bring covenant breaking, adultery, divorce, broken

agreements, broken contracts and not keeping promises.

- **A SPIRIT OF NUMBNESS** is assigned to bring emotional issues, such as moodiness, depression, self-rejection, self-hatred and delusions.
- **A SPIRIT OF PREY** is assigned to bring a victim mentality, being passive, a "poor me" attitude, loneliness, expecting failure, doubt, hopelessness and feelings of unworthiness.
- **A SPIRIT OF PSYCHIATRIC DISORDER** is assigned to bring mental illnesses, such as bipolar disorders, personality disorders, obsessive-compulsive disorders, autistic disorders, schizophrenia and even substance abuse disorders.

Pray and ask God to show you if any of these apply to you. If any *do* apply, ask Him to set you free from such curses.

CHAPTER 11

UNDERSTANDING FAMILIAR SPIRITS

Leviticus 19:31

Regard not them that have familiar spirits, neither seek after wizards, to be defiled by them: I am the LORD your God.

The King James version of the Bible uses the phrase *familiar spirit* sixteen times. The literal translation of the Hebrew words is "knowing spirit." Following are some key facts that you should know about familiar spirits:

- A familiar spirit is an evil spirit that becomes familiar with an individual or family. It follows that person or family and knows their weaknesses—physically, mentally, spiritually and emotionally.
- A familiar spirit cannot read your mind or know your thoughts, but it does know a lot about you.
- A spirit that is familiar with you will communicate knowledge about you to those they serve. Not every person who has supernatural knowledge about you is of God, as we see in Acts when Paul and Silas were imprisoned:

Acts 16:16-18

And it came to pass, as we went to prayer, a certain damsel possessed with a spirit of divination met us, which brought her masters much gain by soothsaying: the same followed Paul and us, and cried, saying, These men are the servants of the most high God, which shew unto us the way of salvation. And this did she many days. But Paul, being grieved, turned and said to the spirit, I command thee in the name of Jesus Christ to come out of her. And he came out the same hour.

If someone, such as a psychic, tells you things about your life that they had no natural way of knowing, there's a good chance that a familiar spirit is in operation.

A familiar spirit is also familiar with an individual's or a family's sins. It knows what buttons to push and what to magnify with each family member. It knows every weakness and almost everything about each family member and uses this knowledge to influence each of them to sin in the area of their individual weakness.

The *modus operandi* of a familiar spirit is to watch and wait for a sin which introduces an open door. Through sin, a curse is then passed on. A familiar spirit can be with a family for generations. It is passed on to future generations who also sin, which allows the same spirit to transcend several generations.

My paternal grandfather was an alcoholic, and my father and his brother were both alcoholics. The spirits of escape watched me through the years. They knew that I was susceptible to a desire to escape reality. I had the potential to get overwhelmed by alcohol and drugs to dull my reality.

I, therefore, inherited a weakness for alcohol and drugs, the spirit of *pharmakeia*. This spirit will be ready to attack my children and generations that follow in years to come. They try to get each generation involved in the same sin, so they can carry the curse on and on.

This does not mean that my children or grandchild are predestined to become alcoholics. It only means that they have a predisposition and may be tempted. Whether or not they respond to those temptations will be their choice. They can choose not to try to escape reality. Personally, I am confident that the curse of alcoholism has been broken with me.

Spirits that control the parents frequently control the children, and many times the manifestations of the stronghold are much worse in the succeeding generations. Demon control can grow with each passing generation.

The Old Testament warns us about familiar spirits:

Leviticus 19:31

Regard not them that have familiar spirits, neither seek after wizards, to be defiled by them: I am the LORD your God.

Leviticus 20:6

And the soul that turneth after such as have familiar spirits, and after wizards, to go a whoring after them, I will even set my face against that soul, and will cut him off from among his people.

Many people consult mediums, clairvoyants and spirits to gain knowledge about their future. They think they are receiving information from the spirit of a loved one or from the spirit of a person who has passed from this life. But no one can call up the spirit of a deceased person except Jesus Christ. The spirit that has been conjured up by someone in the occult practice of necromancy is an evil, lying spirit.

This spirit may know things about your past, but it cannot predict the future. It may know things about you or your circumstances, but that is what a familiar spirit is all about. It will give you enough truth to hook you into thinking it is good. Then it will feed you lies to destroy you.

There is no such thing as a "good" familiar spirit. This truth is confirmed by the following scripture passages:

1 Corinthians 5:3

For I verily, as absent in body, but present in spirit, have judged already, as though I were present, concerning him that hath so done this deed.

2 Corinthians 5:6

Therefore we are always confident, knowing that, whilst we are at home in the body, we are absent from the Lord.

2 Corinthians 5:8

We are confident, I say, and willing rather to be absent from the body, and to be present with the Lord.

This is according to Matt Slick, President and Founder of the Christian Apologetics and Research Ministry. [9]

First Samuel 28 addresses the famous story of Saul and the medium who contacted the spirit of Samuel after he had died. Commentators are split on whether this was actually Samuel or not. Whatever the case, Saul was rebuked for his sin:

9. https://carm.org/what-is-a-familiar-spirit

Leviticus 19:31

Regard not them that have familiar spirits, neither seek after wizards, to be defiled by them: I am the LORD your God.

1 Chronicles 10:13

So Saul died for his transgression which he committed against the LORD, even against the word of the LORD, which he kept not, and also for asking counsel of one that had a familiar spirit, to inquire of it.

The following generations had to deal with the result of Saul's sin:

2 Chronicles 33:1 and 6

Manasseh was twelve years old when he began to reign.

And he caused his children to pass through the fire in the valley of the son of Hinnom: also he observed times, and used enchantments, and used witchcraft, and dealt with a familiar spirit, and with wizards: he wrought much evil in the sight of the LORD, to provoke him to anger.

The God's Word Translation of the Bible says it this way:

2 Chronicles 33:6, GW

He burned his son as a sacrifice in the valley of Ben Hinnom, consulted fortunetellers, cast evil spells, practiced witchcraft, and appointed royal mediums and psychics. He did many things that made the LORD *furious.*

Don't be guilty of playing around with familiar spirits. And, if your family has inherited such spirits, seek deliverance from them immediately.

CHAPTER 12

WHAT DOES A FAMILY CURSE LOOK LIKE?

Proverbs 26:2

As the bird by wandering, as the swallow by flying, so the curse causeless shall not come.

Family curses are reoccurring problems that steal, kill and destroy members of a particular family. As we have seen, the Scriptures are clear that God visits the iniquity of the fathers upon the children up to the third and fourth generation, but curses never visit a family without a cause. When someone in the family tree gives a spirit the right to visit (because of their iniquity), that spirit enters the family tree and waits for every opportunity to affect your life. The good news is this: once family curses are exposed, Christ's deliverance is readily available.

Matthew Henry's Concise Commentary on the Whole Bible (MHCC) [10] states, "He that is cursed without cause, the curse shall do him no more harm than the bird that flies over his head. The curse will fly away like the sparrow and return to its proper place. The proper place is upon the head of the person that sent it. A curse can never take effect on an innocent person.

"You cannot choose your relatives any more than you can choose skin color, gender or race. Someone up the family tree could be the cause for a generational curse. A family curse is a payment or recompense for iniquity. It is written in Lamentations:

Lamentations 3:64-66

Render unto them a recompence, O Lord, according to the work of their hands. Give them sorrow of heart, thy curse unto them. Persecute and destroy them in anger from under the heavens of the Lord.

10. Packard Technologies

Before you can break generational curses, you need to identify their character. Here is a partial list of family curses for your review. Having one of these in your life or family may not indicate a family curse, but to have several reoccurring ones might. The Holy Spirit can help you identify a family curse. As you read this list, ask Him to give you the spirit of revelation to determine if any apply to you and your family.

EMOTIONAL INSTABILITY AND FEAR

Deuteronomy 28:28

The LORD shall smite thee with madness, and blindness, and astonishment of heart:

Notice that this scripture says, "The Lord shall smite thee with madness." To be smitten with madness means insanity, craziness, foolishness or irrational behavior. This verse also uses the term *blindness*. This *blindness* releases confusion and indecision.

The curse follows that with *"astonishment of heart."* This is the same as surprised, bewildered or shocked. Under this curse, one is easily overcome by emotions and fear. These cause a person to make foolish decisions and do crazy self-destructive things. In this condition, a person has a continual inner struggle, internal warfare and frustration.

Confusion and depression are two significant indicators of this family curse. This shows why some are double-minded and have problems ordering their lives by renewing their minds with the Word of God.

HEREDITARY FAMILY SICKNESSES

Some family sicknesses are reoccurring, which may be an indication of a family curse:

Deuteronomy 28:21-22

The LORD shall make the pestilence cleave to thee, until he shall have consumed thee from off the land, whither thou goest to possess it. The LORD shall smite thee with a consumption, and with a fever, and with an inflammation, and with an extreme burning, and with the sword, and with blasting, and with mildew; and they shall pursue thee until thou perish.

Notice the terms *pestilence* and *consumption*. This curse releases sicknesses of all kinds. Consumption is a wasting lung diseases like emphysema, COPD and lung cancer. This passage also uses terms *fever* and *inflammation*. These indicate a curse that is evidenced by arthritis. Inflammation of the brain can lead to Alzheimer's disease.

Next, we see the term *extreme burning*. This refers to all sorts of venereal diseases and infections.

THE BOTCH

Deuteronomy 28:27

The Lord will smite thee with the botch of Egypt, and with hemorrhoids, and with the scab, and with the itch, of which thou canst not be healed.

Botches are open sores or boils. These are experienced by those who have problems with wounds that will not heal. The Scriptures also say:

Deuteronomy 28:35

The Lord shall smite thee in the knees, and in the

legs, with a sore botch that cannot be healed, from the sole of thy foot unto the top of thy head.

This curse attacks legs, the soles of the feet and the top of one's head. In fact, the Lord didn't leave any diseases out of this curse. He declared:

Deuteronomy 28:61

Also every sickness, and every plague, which is not written in the book of this law, them will the LORD bring upon thee until thou be destroyed.

BARRENNESS, IMPOTENCE AND FEMALE PROBLEMS

Deuteronomy 28:18

Cursed shall be the fruit of thy body, and the fruit of thy land, the increase of thy kine, and the flocks of thy sheep.

Menstrual problems may be the result of a family curse. The Scriptures say, "*Cursed shall be the fruit of thy body.*"

The Hebrew word translated here as *body* is *beten*, which means "womb, belly or abdomen." The womb deals with reproduction. Signs of this curse are infections, hormonal problems, menstrual problems, PMS, cramps, fibroid tissues, painful sex, barrenness, miscarriages, cysts, tumors, bladder problems and kidney stones. Female problems plague millions of women. Men, too can, manifest this curse with erectile dysfunction and impotence.

FAMILY BREAKDOWNS, DIVORCE

Deuteronomy 28:30

Thou shalt betroth a wife, and another man shall lie with her: thou shalt build a house, and thou shalt not dwell therein: thou shalt plant a vineyard, and shalt not gather the grapes thereof.

This curse manifests in several ways and includes: divorce, family division, fights among relatives, families that scatter, have no fellowship, or have jailed children and estranged relationships.

Obviously, children are also affected by this family curse:

Deuteronomy 28:32

Thy sons and thy daughters shall be given unto another people, and thine eyes shall look, and fail with longing for them all the day long: and there shall be no might in thine hand.

Deuteronomy 28:41

Thou shalt beget sons and daughters, but thou shalt not enjoy them; for they shall go into captivity.

The iniquities of the fathers are visited upon the children. Here are some statistics of family breakdowns affecting children today:

- Since 1980, the marriage rate is down about 45%.
- 41% of children are born to unmarried mothers (73% for African-Americans). [11]
- 71% of poor couples are not married. [12]

---

11. Center for Disease Control, National Vital Statistics, 2009.
12. Robert Rector, "*Marriage: America's Greatest Weapon Against Child Poverty,*" Heritage Foundation, 2010, http://www.heritage.org/research/reports/2010/09/marriage-america-sgreatest-weapon-against-child-poverty.

- Marriage decreases by 82% the probability that a child will live in poverty. [13]

Fatherless or single-parent homes produce children who are:

- Two times more likely to be arrested for juvenile crime. [14]
- Two times more likely to be treated for emotional and behavioral problems. [15]
- Two times more likely to be suspended or expelled from school.[16]
- Thirty-three percent more likely to drop out of school. [17]
- Three times more likely to end up in jail by age 30. [18]

---

13. Ibid
14. Chris Coughlin and Samuel Vuchinich, "Family Experience in Preadolescence and the Development of Male Delinquency," Journal of Marriage and Family, vol. 58, no. 2 (1996): 491–501.
15. Deborah A. Dawson, "Family Structure and Children's Health and WellBeing: Data from the 1988 National Health Interview Survey on Child Health," Journal of Marriage and Family, vol. 53, no. 3 (August 1991): 573– 584.
16. Wendy D. Manning and Kathleen A. Lamb, "Adolescent Well-Being in Cohabiting Married, and Single-Parent Families," Journal of Marriage and Family, vol. 65, no. 4 (2003): 876–893. Data from Add Health study. See also Dawson, "Family Structure and Children's Health and Well-Being: Data from the 1988 National Health Interview Survey on Child Health."
17. Timothy Biblarz and Greg Gottainer, "Family Structure and Children's Success: A Comparison of Widowed and Divorced Single-Mother Families," Journal of Marriage and Family, vol. 62 (May 2000): 533–548.
18. Trevor Thomas, American Thinker, "The Fatherless Effect", https://www.ameri-

LACK, POVERTY AND THE INABILITY TO PRODUCE

Deuteronomy 28:17 and 29

Cursed shall be thy basket and thy store.

And thou shalt grope at noonday, as the blind gropeth in darkness, and thou shalt not prosper in thy ways: and thou shalt be only oppressed and spoiled evermore, and no man shall save thee.

This is a curse on finances, and it affects one's ability to produce. Production gives us the ability for wealth building. Under this curse, one's ability to get wealth is hindered. People under this curse never have anything saved. They are continually oppressed by bill collectors, and what little they accumulate is stolen by the spoilers.

BEING PERPETUALLY IN DEBT, POVERTY

Deuteronomy 28:48

Therefore shalt thou serve thine enemies which the LORD *shall send against thee, in hunger, and in*

canthinker.com/articles/2016/07/the_fatherless_effect.html#ixzz5YxyVkp59 *thirst, and in nakedness, and in want of all things: and he shall put a yoke of iron upon thy neck, until he have destroyed thee.*

These same people are slaves to their creditors, and this family curse of lack and poverty needs to be broken. God's promise is:

2 Corinthians 9:8

And God is able to make all grace abound toward you; that ye, always having all sufficiency in all things, may abound to every good work.

Poverty is not having what you need to do God's will. It is not a blessing from God to not have the means to accomplish His plan for your life. A person under this curse will misuse and waste what they have and go further in debt and bondage. They are candidates for get-rich-quick schemes of all kinds. The blessed man is not focused on material wealth, but on fulfilling his purpose in life, as he keeps and follows the commandments of the Lord, putting the Kingdom of God and His righteousness first in everything (see Matthew 6:33).

NO AMBITION, VISION OR DIRECTION

Deuteronomy 28:29

And thou shalt grope at noonday as the blind gropeth in darkness, and thou shalt not prosper in thy ways: and thou shalt be only oppressed and spoiled evermore, and no man shall save thee.

There are those who have no internal vision for their lives. They set no goals, and are blown to and fro by life's circumstances. This curse is revealed in those without ambition. They go aimlessly through life.

Ambition is a strong desire to make a difference with your life. It's a vision, dream or aspiration to succeed. Those under this curse are careless about tomorrow. They are without hope and terribly negative. They *"grope"* as *"blind men"* with no direction, always uncertain and full of apathy and lukewarmness.

We have learned, however, that curses don't visit the family without cause. Someone in the family tree could have been the originator of this curse. Breaking family curses requires you to think about what reoccurring things attack your family. By now, I am sure, the Holy Spirit has shown you some possibilities.

We know that our generational curses have been broken in Jesus' name, but it is still good to verbally confess, repent and declare your freedom. As noted in Chapter 6, there is power in our verbal confessions.

If you are unsure of whether or not a curse should be broken, I recommend breaking it anyway, just so you know it's broken. It doesn't hurt to break a curse that's already been broken. Here's a sample prayer you can pray that you can use to break yourself free from spoken generational curses:

In the name of Jesus, and by the power of His blood, I now renounce, break and sever all curses that have been handed down to me from my ancestors. In the name of Jesus, I now loose myself and my future generations from any bondages passed down to me from my ancestors!

Amen!

CHAPTER 13

DEALING WITH A SPIRIT OF LUST AND PERVERSION

Isaiah 19:14

The Lord *hath mingled a perverse spirit in the midst thereof: and they have caused Egypt to err in every work thereof, as a drunken man staggereth in his vomit.*

Spirits of lust will cause a strong, irresistible urge to commit sexual sin. These spirits can make it miserable on the person to resist those types of sins because of the intense pressure that is put on them. A person can be delivered by casting out the spirits. Once the spirit is commanded out, the person is relieved from such pressure and the tendency to sin. When they are being controlled by a spirit, they are driven and pressured from within. In a normal situation, without being influenced by a spirit would be more like being tempted from the outside.

A person who has a spirit of lust or perversion, will feel an unusually strong attraction toward sexual desires. Somebody who has a spirit of addiction will often find it very hard to break off from whatever they are addicted to, and if they do break off, they will soon become addicted to something else. For example, they will exchange a bondage to smoking for an eating disorder, or addiction to M&M candy to peanuts and jelly beans.

Dictionary.com defines *perversion* as "any of various means of obtaining sexual gratification that are generally regarded as being abnormal; pathology, a change to what is unnatural or abnormal." [19] My definition of perversion is "the condition characterized by sexually abnormal and unacceptable practices or corrupt tendencies. It is the moving away from the natural to

19. https://www.dictionary.com/browse/perversion

unnatural sexual practices or acts especially when it is done habitually."

The spirit of perversion can be manifested in many ways, such as sexual perversions, child abuse, pornography, incest and having a filthy mind.

Perversion is not always sexual. In addition to sex, perversion may manifest in other ways. Chronic worrying, walking in foolishness, twisting the Word of God, evil actions, abortion, doctrinal error and skepticism also fall under the heading of perversion.

In the book of Isaiah, God allowing a perverse spirit to be circulated in the midst of Egypt because of their continual sin and disobedience to Him. Because of man's disobedience and rebellion against God and His Word, He will allow a perverse spirit to take over the minds and hearts of those who embrace and welcome such a spirit.

When we obey God and His Word, we reap abundant life, blessings, protection, joy, peace, love and everything good that God has purposed for our lives. When we go against His Word and will in rebellion and choose to live life our way, we reap sorrow and pain, hurt, confusion, lack, poverty and even death.

Disobedience always leads to perversion. In Romans 1, we can see how our disobedience can and will lead to a spirit of perversion taking over our lives:

Romans 1:18-32

For the wrath of God is revealed from heaven against all ungodliness and unrighteousness of men, who hold the truth in unrighteousness; because that which may be known of God is manifest in them; for God hath shewed it unto them. For the invisible things of him from the creation of the world are clearly seen, being understood by the things that are made, even his eternal power and Godhead; so that they are without excuse:

Because that, when they knew God, they glorified him not as God, neither were thankful; but became vain in their imaginations, and their foolish heart was darkened. Professing themselves to be wise, they became fools, and changed the glory of the uncorruptible God into an image made like to corruptible man, and to birds, and four footed beasts, and creeping things.

Wherefore God also gave them up to uncleanness through the lusts of their own hearts, to dishonour their own bodies between themselves: who changed the truth of God into a lie, and worshipped and served the creature more than the Creator, who is blessed forever. Amen.

For this cause God gave them up unto vile affections: for even their women did change the natural use into that which is against nature: And likewise also the men, leaving the natural use of the woman, burned in their lust one toward another; men with men working that which is unseemly, and receiving in themselves that recompence of their error which was meet.

And even as they did not like to retain God in their knowledge, God gave them over to a reprobate mind, to do those things which are not convenient; being filled with all unrighteousness, fornication, wickedness, covetousness, maliciousness; full of envy, murder, debate, deceit, malignity; whisperers, backbiters, haters of God, despiteful, proud, boasters, inventors of evil things, disobedient to parents, without understanding, covenant breakers, without natural affection, implacable, unmerciful: Who knowing the judgment of God, that they which commit such things are worthy of death, not only do the same, but have pleasure in them that do them.

The New Living Translation makes it a bit clearer:

Romans 1:18-32, NLT

But God shows his anger from heaven against all sinful, wicked people who suppress the truth by their wickedness. They know the truth about God because he has made it obvious to them. For ever since the world was created, people have seen the earth and sky. Through everything God made, they can clearly see his invisible qualities—his eternal power and divine nature. So they have no excuse for not knowing God.

Yes, they knew God, but they wouldn't worship him as God or even give him thanks. And they began to think up foolish ideas of what God was like. As a result, their minds became dark and confused. Claiming to be wise, they instead became utter fools. And instead of worshiping the glorious, everliving God, they worshiped idols made to look like mere people and birds and animals and reptiles.

So God abandoned them to do whatever shameful things their hearts desired. As a result, they did vile and degrading things with each other's bodies. They traded the truth about God for a lie. So they worshiped and served the things God created instead of the Creator himself, who is worthy of eternal praise! Amen. That is why God abandoned them to their shameful desires. Even the women turned against the natural way to have sex and instead indulged in sex with each other. And the men, instead of having normal sexual relations with women, burned with lust for each other. Men did shameful things with other men, and as a result of this sin, they suffered within themselves the penalty they deserved.

Since they thought it foolish to acknowledge God, he abandoned them to their foolish thinking and let them do things that should never be done. Their lives became full of every kind of wickedness, sin, greed, hate, envy, murder, quarreling, deception, malicious behavior, and gossip. They are backstabbers, haters of God, insolent, proud, and boastful. They invent new ways of sinning, and they disobey their parents. They refuse to understand, break their promises, are heartless, and have no mercy. They know God's justice requires that those who do these things deserve to die, yet they do them anyway. Worse yet, they encourage others to do them, too.

As a result of disobedience, the lives of these people became full of every kind of perversion: wickedness, sin, greed, hate, envy, murder, quarreling, deception, malicious behavior and gossip.

Satan works through an evil spirit within a person, with the intent to destroy their life with sexual addictions. Some of the more common ways are: pornography, masturbation and unnatural sexual desires. Lustful addictions destroy people's lives, marriages and families.

Masturbation brings guilt and shame upon a person. Sexual abuse and rape can cause the victim to open the door of their emotions to even worse spirits. Then spirits such as hate, anger, shame, distrust etc., can come in and take up residence in their emotional realm. As we have seen, God's Word warns us not to let Satan gain an advantage over our emotions.

It matters not which spirit overcomes an individual, with the command of authority, by the blood of Jesus Christ, it can and must be cast out.

CHAPTER 14

DEALING WITH A SPIRIT OF ANTAGONISM

James 4:7

Submit yourselves therefore to God. Resist the devil, and he will flee from you.

A spirit of antagonism brings with it spirits of anger, hate and rage. This spirit causes uncontrolled anger-related weaknesses in a person. King Saul was a prime example. Once an evil spirit entered him, he became fierce and even tried to kill David.

Anger is a leading cause of damaged marriages, abused children and violence in the home, school and workplace. Unresolved anger is one of the chief contributing factors to the destruction of marriages, the breakdown of families and the weakening of communities. It is a major cause of health problems and a lack of productivity in the workplace, and is also a common denominator among juvenile delinquents.

One root cause of a spirit of anger is tension from past hurts and guilt. This mixture of pain and guilt is cumulative, and it erupts in anger when new offenses remind us of past experiences. Most people assume that hurtful events in the past will be forgotten and will have no effect on their future. That is not always true. Past hurts do not just go away on their own; nor does guilt simply disappear after a wrong response to a situation. Unless these experiences are resolved through repentance and forgiveness, we may continue to experience fits of anger when our pressure points are triggered.

Anger is a gateway. It leads to bitterness, and where we typically lash out in wrath, revenge or other hurtful responses. In this way, encounters from the past shape our current experiences

THE PAIN OF REJECTION

The pain of rejection is one of the strongest factors in a person's life, especially in childhood. A child forms strong attachment to parents, friends and relatives and finds security in these relationships. When someone communicates rejection, the child's secure world collapses, and he faces a host of fears. The pain of rejection and the torment of fears can cause a child to develop a deep bitterness toward the one who is responsible for his pain.

When parents are divorced, their children typically experience the pain of rejection, whatever their age.

THE REACTION TO UNCHANGEABLE FEATURES OF OUR LIVES

One of the greatest challenges facing each of us is that of accepting unchangeable features, such as physical appearance, mental capabilities, birth order, race, brothers and sisters or parents. When someone mocks or ridicules a person who is already insecure, it is a devastating blow to his self-esteem. Ridicule does not just attack a person's actions; it hits at his very personhood. One who experiences ridicule will become extremely sensitive.

THE GRIEF OF FAVORITISM

When parents favor one child over another, they are not only damaging the self-worth of a child who is less appreciated; they are also encouraging him or her to react toward the one who is favored. Favoritism to one will be received as rejection by the other.

Jacob's favoritism of Joseph over the rest of his sons is a typical example of this situation (see Genesis 37:3). Joseph's brothers resented the favor Joseph received, and the result was that they hated him and eventually sold him into slavery.

THE ANGUISH OF FALSE ACCUSATIONS

A person's reputation has great worth. Solomon wrote:

Proverbs 22:1

A good name is rather to be chosen than great riches, and loving favour rather than silver and gold.

A false accusation not only damages the one who is accused; it also stirs up resentment and a desire to see the false accuser brought to justice. The mixture of guilt and pain that surrounds the memory of such experiences triggers anger when we hear of or face similar situations.

Can you recall a past experience that deeply hurt you? How do similar situations cause you to express anger now? [20] You can determine attitudes and actions that open the door to a spirit of anger. Along with painful experiences, our own tendencies foster a spirit of anger. The following attitudes and actions lead to guilt and anger:

PRIDE

Pride is assuming authority that does not belong to us. Many conflicts arise simply because we step into another's jurisdiction with efforts to control. No wonder others react to us in this situation. In turn, the rejection we experience as a result can then lead to more expressions of anger (which are often accompanied by bitterness).

---

20. This information adapted from p 6, 38–40 of the Anger Resolution Seminar Workbook https://iblp.org/discipleship-tools/anger-resolution-seminar

PERSONAL FAULTS

When we fail in specific areas, we tend to be very alert to other people who fail in those same areas. Unfortunately, the frustration we have toward ourselves is often redirected at others through harsh judgment. Also, when someone hurts or offends us, his or her actions may be partially justified, which can trigger an explosive combination of guilt and bitterness in us.

GENERALIZATIONS

If someone who represents another group or race hurts us, we tend to project the misbehavior of one onto the entire group and often develop a general animosity toward everyone who is associated with that group.

EXPECTATIONS

When people make promises and fail to keep them, we tend to hold that against them and become resentful of their failure to fulfill our expectations. When we expect certain behavior or benefits from others, especially those who are closest to us, and they do not act as we expect, resentment can also occur.

ENVY

Envy is bitterness toward another person who has received something we want and think we deserve. Envy is a form of anger that might not be obvious to others until something triggers an angry outburst or reaction by the envious person.

TAKING UP OFFENSES

One of the most entangling causes of bitterness occurs when a person who was not directly involved in an offensive situation takes up an offense on behalf of the one who was offended. This kind of bitterness is deep-seated and often endures even after the one who was offended forgives the offender. [21]

When we become angry, we should identify the past experiences and personal failures that are contributing to our current frustration and seek to resolve them. Often, situations that are like ones in which we were hurt or failed to do the right thing will trigger our anger. Usually the stronger the anger, the more pain and guilt there are from the past.

21. Ibid

Paul was inspired to write:

Ephesians 4:25-26, 29-32, GW

"Be angry without sinning. Don't go to bed angry. Don't give the devil any opportunity to work. Don't say anything that would hurt another person. Instead, speak only what is good so that you can give help wherever it is needed. That way, what you say will help those who hear you. Don't give God's Holy Spirit any reason to be upset with you. He has put his seal on you for the day you will be set free from the world of sin. Get rid of your bitterness, hot tempers, anger, loud quarreling, cursing, and hatred. Be kind to each other, sympathetic, forgiving each other as God has forgiven you through Christ.

It is not normal to have an ongoing bondage to anger. God's Word tells us that if we resist the devil and draw near to God, the devil will have to flee:

James 4:7

Submit yourselves therefore to God. Resist the devil, and he will flee from you.

This scripture is speaking of normal temptations that come from the outside. It is not talking about internal bondages, which involve demons that need to be cast out. Having a demon sets a person up for pressure to fail. The demon is a driving force within you that does not leave, even after it has been resisted and you've drawn near to God. In this case, it's quite possible that an unclean spirit needs to be cast out.

The goal of casting out a spirit of antagonism is to relieve the person of the severe pressure they are feeling, which is trying to make them angry. When the root issues in the people's life is dealt with and the demons cast out, true and lasting freedom becomes a reality.

Chapter 15

DEALING WITH A SPIRIT OF SELF-HATRED

Ecclesiastes 2:17-18

Therefore I hated life; because the work that is wrought under the sun is grievous unto me: for all is vanity and vexation of spirit. Yea, I hated all my labour which I had taken under the sun: because I should leave it unto the man that shall be after me.

Self-imposed bondages such as self-hate, self-rejection, etc. are among Satan's favorite tools. Knowing who you are in Christ is vital to your spiritual growth, healing and deliverance. If you have a problem in this area of your life, the process of inner healing and deliverance can be hindered. Therefore, overcoming this roadblock is essential to moving forward smoothly and efficiently in working with the other bondages in your life.

Bob Larson, a well-respected name in deliverance ministry, has an MP4 download entitled "Six Strongholds of Satan" that addresses the six strongholds of Satan. He explains that it's not in Satanism, witchcraft and those other heavier areas where Satan is commonly found. The most common issues of unresolved emotions, such as fear, anger, rejection, depression, self-hatred and abuse can be doorways to the soul. [22]

Rejection is one of the main forces that push people into Satanism. Rebellion and insecurity are among the forces that push people into witchcraft. They get into witchcraft because they desire to have power over another individual, to manipulate and control them.

There is also what I call "white witchcraft." This is a desire to have power, to manipulate and have control over another person's will. Using scripture and

---

22. https://www.boblarson.org/webstore/product/six-strongholds-of-satan-mp4download/

praying a selfish desire that benefits you, rather than the Father's will qualifies for white witchcraft.

White Witchcraft is a practice believed to provide good intentions to the people around you. The practitioners are often said to have a Wiccan faith. Wicca is a religion which is guided by modern pagan beliefs. The practitioners of Wicca normally utilize prayers and rituals. They use spells to attempt to control and manipulate others.

The doorways to Satanism, witchcraft and the heavier areas that Satan exploits are rejection, insecurity, rebellion, self-hatred and unforgiveness.

In Black Witchcraft, practitioners perform acts which are spiteful and provide harm to others. They utilize unnatural acts which inflict damage to other people. They conduct negative acts to spitefully punish their enemies for their own selfish gain.

Satan wants us to hate ourselves. In the ministry of deliverance, self-hatred is huge. Not only is it very popular, but it is also very destructive. Self-hatred, the tendency to hate ourselves, is always spiritually destructive. We cannot truly love others, unless we first truly love ourselves. And, if we fail to love others, then we are not keeping the commandment of Jesus, to love one another. Satan wants our thinking to be in complete disagreement with God's thinking about who we are.

Satan causes low self-worth, often referred to as low self-esteem. He will use guilt, false humility and dead religious thinking to cause us to look down upon ourselves. I would like to ask the questions: "Have you been listening to the devil?" and, if so, "Have you been basing your identity upon what he's been telling you?"

It is absolutely essential to know that you are forgiven. As long as you question your status with God, the healing process is being held back.

Did you know that false guilt and a failure to forgive yourself are things Satan will use against you? The reason so many cannot seem to break free from guilt is that they have failed to forgive themselves.

When we forgive ourselves, as God has forgiven us, the guilt that Satan has been pushing on us disappears. However, when we fail to forgive ourselves, this failure to forgive ourselves turns into self-hate, and this bondage becomes like a snowball rolling down a hill.

Both the failure to forgive ourselves and false guilt deny the work that Christ has done for us on the cross. Therefore, learning how to forgive yourself so that you can break free from false guilt is vital to becoming the person Christ created you to be.

Many marriages and relationships are destroyed because of self-hatred. When a person does not respect themselves, they will lose respect for others and, ultimately, for God Himself. The truth is that we can only genuinely love others when we first love ourselves.

A good way for a believer to guard against self-hatred is to learn what God says about you in His Word. As an example, He said:

Jeremiah 29:11

For I know the thoughts that I think toward you, saith the Lord, thoughts of peace, and not of evil, to give you an expected end.

If God has good thoughts about you, why should you have any other thought. Learn the many more good things God's Word says about you, and that will help you prevent the enemy from gaining a foothold in your thoughts.

God has also said:

Proverbs 15:32

He that refuseth instruction despiseth his own soul: but he that heareth reproof getteth understanding.

Accept His instruction, and you will close the door to Satan's attempts to gain access to your life.

CHAPTER 16

TRACING GENERATIONAL INIQUITY

Nehemiah 9:2

And the seed of Israel separated themselves from all strangers, and stood and confessed their sins, and the iniquities of their fathers

As we have noted, we are not held responsible for the sins of our ancestors, but we are susceptible to their areas of weakness and should be alert to these inclinations. Looking back to our parents, grandparents, and great-grandparents, we can often trace certain physical features, strengths and weaknesses through the family line. In the same way, we can observe character traits and spiritual influences that span the generations.

A godly heritage offers a strong foundation of virtue and faithfulness, but conducts such as anger, lust and bitterness set destructive patterns that need to be recognized and overcome.

In the biblical account of Abraham's family, the iniquity of deception became a stronghold that affected the lives of Abraham, then Isaac, then Jacob and then Jacob's sons (see Genesis 12:11–13 and 26:7-8).

Genesis 12:11-13

And it came to pass, when he was come near to enter into Egypt, that he said unto Sarai his wife, Behold now, I know that thou art a fair woman to look upon: therefore it shall come to pass, when the Egyptians shall see thee, that they shall say, This is his wife: and they will kill me, but they will save thee alive. Say, I pray thee, thou art my sister: that it may be well with me for thy sake; and my soul shall live because of thee.

The suggestion of Abraham to Sarah about what she should say was true in words, but it was a deception, intended to give an impression that she was no more than his sister. In actuality, Abraham was lying and twisting the truth. According to *Matthew Henry's Commentary*, this was "a great fault which Abram was guilty of, in denying his wife and pretending that she was his sister. His fault was misleading others about his relation to Sarah, equivocating concerning it and teaching his wife, and probably all his attendants, to do so too. What he said was, in a sense, true, but with a purpose to deceive."

To justify himself, Abraham said:

Genesis 20:12

And yet indeed she is my sister; she is the daughter of my father, but not the daughter of my mother; and she became my wife.

Matthew Henry continued: "He [Abraham] so concealed a further truth as in effect to deny it, and to expose thereby both his wife and the Egyptians to sin. That which was at the bottom of it was a jealous nervous fancy he had that some of the Egyptians would be so charmed with the beauty of Sarah that, if they should know he was her husband, they would find some way or other to take him off, that they might marry her."

Amazingly, the exact same thing later happened to Isaac, Abraham's son and Isaac's wife, Rebekah:

Genesis 26:6-8

And Isaac dwelt in Gerar: and the men of the place asked him of his wife; and he said, She is my sister: for he feared to say, She is my wife; lest, said he, the men of the place should kill me for Rebekah; because she was fair to look upon. And it came to pass, when he had been there a long time, that Abimelech king of the Philistines looked out at a window, and saw, and, behold, Isaac was sporting with Rebekah his wife.

Like his father before him, Isaac lied and twisted the truth. According to Matthew Henry, "Isaac had now laid aside all thoughts of going to Egypt, and, in obedience to the heavenly vision, set up his staff in

Gerar, the country in which he was born. Still, there he entered into temptation, the same temptation that his good father had been once and again surprised and overcome by, namely, to deny his wife, and to give out that she was his sister. Because his wife was handsome, he fancied the Philistines would find some way or other to take him off, that some of them might marry her; and therefore she must pass for his sister. It is an unaccountable thing that both these great and good men should be guilty of so strange a piece of dissimulation, by which they so much exposed both their own and their wives' reputation."

When we understand how our lives are influenced by our forefathers, we can respond appropriately to that influence. We should acknowledge the iniquities of our forefathers, repent of our own sins and endeavor to overcome the tendencies toward specific sins that we have inherited.

Consider these passages:

Nehemiah 9:2

And the seed of Israel separated themselves from all strangers, and stood and confessed their sins, and the iniquities of their fathers

Daniel 9:16

O Lord, according to all thy righteousness, I beseech thee, let thine anger and thy fury be turned away from thy city Jerusalem, thy holy mountain: because for our sins, and for the iniquities of our fathers, Jerusalem and thy people are become a reproach to all that are about us.

Jeremiah 14:20

We acknowledge, O Lord, our wickedness, and the iniquity of our fathers: for we have sinned against thee.

Confess your own sins first, assuming personal responsibility for them. Then know that you will never experience the freedom Jesus promises as long as there is iniquity or unconfessed sin in your family. Therefore take an inventory to see if there are demonic strongholds (iniquities) in your life or the lives of other family members.

Overwhelming evidence has shown that the ruling spirits involved in strongholds attract certain individuals to each other. Rejection attracts rejection, rebellion attracts rebellion and so forth. The people involved are comfortable with each other. I have listed below a few strongholds in which iniquities have been passed down from generation to generation. These represent different demonic strongholds. I have also included the symptoms commonly produced when a stronghold is present and is affecting your life.

Consider each warning sign that is habitually present in your life. When considering these, assess the intensity of influence and control the symptom has over you. Please note that the symptom must be habitually present, not just a passing feeling or an occasional situation.

- **The spirit of deceit** is a ruling spirit which can be identified by the following behaviors: lying, fantasies, delusions, rationalizations, wrong doctrines and the misuse of scripture.
- **The spirit of confusion** is a ruling spirit which can be identified by the following behaviors: doubt, unbelief, suspicion, apprehension, indecision, skepticism and being unsettled.

- **The spirit of dependence** is a ruling spirit which may be identified by the following behaviors: insensitivity, loneliness, self-determination, over-confidence, withdrawal, excuse-making and lack of trust.
- **The spirit of control** is a ruling spirit which may be identified by the following behaviors: manipulation, lacking trust, desiring recognition and violence.
- **The spirit of witchcraft/familiar spirit** is a ruling spirit which may be identified by the following behaviors: blasphemy and rebelliousness.
- **The spirit of bitterness** is a ruling spirit which may be identified by the following behaviors: resentment, racism, unforgiveness, anger/hatred, violence and revenge
- **The spirit of rejection** is a ruling spirit which may be identified by the following behaviors: addictive behaviors, compulsions, seeking acceptance, feelings of unworthiness, withdrawal and thoughts of suicide.
- **The spirit of lust** is a ruling spirit which may be identified by the following behaviors:

chronic grumbling, seductiveness, masturbation, fornication, adultery, homosexuality and pornography.

- **The spirit of heaviness** is a ruling spirit which may be identified by the following behaviors: depression, despair, self-pity and loneliness.
- **The spirit of pride** is a ruling spirit which may be identified by the following behaviors: self-righteousness, self-centeredness, materialism and position seeking.
- **The spirit of rebellion** is a ruling spirit which may be identified by the following behaviors: stubbornness, pouting, strife, disruptiveness, independence, indifference and unteachableness.
- **The spirit of jealousy** is a ruling spirit which may be identified by the following behaviors: spitefulness, gossip/slander, betrayal, being critical in nature, judgmental and suspicious.
- **The spirit of fear** is a ruling spirit which may be identified by the following behaviors: insecurity, inferiority, inadequacy and timidity, pleasing people rather than God and dread of failure.

Could any of these be present in your life? How many times have you fought or struggled with a temptation in your own life, doing your best to fight a good fight, but you were still perplexed as to why this thing was even a temptation to you in the first place? How often have you cringed at your own behavior because it reminded you of things that were done, or reactions to situations by your parents, grandparents, other relatives or someone else connected to you by a covenant?

There are two evil forces at work that go mostly undetected in Christian families. They are iniquity and sin. Most people think these two biblical terms are synonymous, but they are not. Sin is "a personal attitude or action in direct rebellion against God's Word." Iniquity is "a wicked act or immoral conduct or practice that is harmful or offensive to God."

David saw the difference:

Psalm 51:2-4

Wash me thoroughly from mine iniquity and cleanse me from my sin. For I acknowledge my transgressions: and my sin is ever before me. Against thee, thee only, have I sinned, and done this evil in thy sight: that thou mightest be justified when thou speakest, and be clear when thou judgest.

The Hebrew word translated *sin* is *chattaah* (H2403) which denotes "an offence, sometimes habitual sinfulness." In verse four here, the Hebrew word translated *sinned* is *chata* (H2398) which denotes "to miss, to forfeit, lack and lead astray." It's like shooting an arrow at a target, and you not only miss the bull's eye; you miss the target altogether. Your arrow falls short, just as we all fall far short of the glory of God.

Romans 3:23

For all have sinned, and come short of the glory of God

The Greek word translated *sin* is *hamartano* (G264), which denotes "to miss the mark and so not share in the prize, and to err."

Psalm 51 mentions iniquity three times.

Psalm 51:2

Wash me thoroughly from mine iniquity, and cleanse me from my sin.

Psalm 51:5

Behold, I was shapen in iniquity; and in sin did my mother conceive me.

Psalm 51:9

Hide thy face from my sins, and blot out all mine iniquities.

The Hebrew word translated *iniquity* here is *avon* (H5771) and denotes "perversity, fault, mischief and punishment." It comes from *avah* (H5753), which is "a primitive root which denotes to crook, bow down, make crooked, pervert, trouble, do wickedly, do wrong and turn." It is the picture of bending over in the same position so frequently that your posture becomes naturally distorted.

All truth is parallel. Committing an act, such as being judgmental so frequently until that act becomes habitual and is rationalized as natural behavior is iniquity. You have heard people say "that is just who he is" to describe someone's conduct. If you repeatedly commit a bad habit, it becomes an iniquity which can be passed down through the bloodline.

When you continually transgress the law, iniquity is created in you, and that iniquity is passed to your children. Your offspring will have a weakness for the same kind of sin.

Each generation adds to the overall iniquity, and every generation is weakened in that area. This will make the iniquity harder to resist. If the family tree is not cleansed of this iniquity, then each generation will become worse and will do what their parents, grandparents and great-grandparents did. The next generation will bend the same way as the past generations. This then becomes a bond of iniquity or a generational curse in that family.

The word *iniquity* means "to bend or to distort the heart." It also implies "a certain weakness or predisposition toward something contrary to God that is passed along from generation to generation in a family."

Isaiah declared that Christ was bruised for our "*iniquities*":

Isaiah 53:5

But he was wounded for our transgressions, he was bruised for our iniquities: the chastisement of our peace was upon him; and with his stripes we are healed.

Yes, Jesus was bruised for our iniquities. Through the bruises He endured on the cross, the provision has been made to restore you and your family to wholeness in the soulish realm, where the mind, will and emotions are located.

The difference between a wound and a bruise is that if you wound yourself, it will eventually scab over and heal. A bruise, however, is deep and can and stay around for a very long time. It may become discolored and can even go so deep as to bruise the bone. An iniquity can be compared to a bruise because it stays around and goes to the bone from generation to generation to generation.

Paul had a revelation on this:

2 Thessalonians 2:7

For the mystery of iniquity doth already work: only he who now letteth will let, until he be taken out of the way.

"The mystery of iniquity" Paul was referring to was the unseen and mysterious connection between a father's sins and the path of his children. As an example, if a father is a liar and a thief, his children are prone to the same behavior.

There are many examples in the Bible of the weakness of iniquity being passed along for generations, as we have seen beginning with Abraham. Fearing King Abimelech, Abraham lied, saying that Sarah was his sister:

Genesis 20:2

And Abraham said of Sarah his wife, She is my sister: and Abimelech king of Gerar sent, and took Sarah.

Abraham's son Isaac, fearing King Abimelech, lied saying that his wife, Rebekah, was his sister:

Genesis 26:6-7

And Isaac dwelt in Gerar: and the men of the place asked him of his wife; and he said, She is my sister: for he feared to say, She is my wife; lest, said he, the men of the place should kill me for Rebekah; because she was fair to look upon.

Desiring his father's blessing, Jacob lied to Isaac, telling him that he was Esau:

Genesis 27:32

And Isaac his father said unto him, Who art thou? And he said, I am thy son, thy firstborn Esau.

Only the iniquities of our forefathers, that is, their predispositions to a particular weakness, are passed along to us, not their sins. The Lord assures us:

Exodus 20:5

Thou shalt not bow down thyself to them, nor serve them: for I the LORD thy God am a jealous God, visiting the iniquity of the fathers upon the children unto the third and fourth generation of them that hate me.

Exodus 34:6-7

And the LORD passed by before him, and proclaimed, The LORD, The LORD God, merciful and gracious, longsuffering, and abundant in goodness and truth, keeping mercy for thousands, forgiving iniquity and transgression and sin, and that will by no means clear the guilty; visiting the iniquity of the fathers upon the children, and upon the children's children, unto the third and to the fourth generation.

Numbers 14:18-19

The LORD is longsuffering, and of great mercy, forgiving iniquity and transgression, and by no means clearing the guilty, visiting the iniquity of the fathers upon the children unto the third and fourth generation. Pardon, I beseech thee, the iniquity of this people according unto the greatness of thy mercy, and as thou hast forgiven this people, from Egypt even until now.

The iniquity of our forefathers is often passed down through generational strongholds that are neither confronted nor renounced and rejected. When we look in the mirror, we see a reflection of our image staring back at us. If we were raised by biological parents or relatives, we can easily see, by comparison, that many of our physical attributes have been passed to us from our parents or grandparents. Even our talents and our likes and dislikes are transferred from our parents or grandparents.

As you were growing up, how you viewed and interacted with the world around you was continually influenced or controlled by the strongholds in your soulish realm (the mind, will and emotions) and the weaknesses within your family. In one family, these weaknesses might be overwhelming feelings of fear and insecurity; in another, rejection; and in still another, bitterness, etc. Through those strongholds, the devil has had a place to operate from within the souls of your family for generations.

But there is great news! You and your entire family and relatives have divine power in Jesus to take back the ground you and your forefathers before you have given over to Satan.

Again, Paul wrote:

Ephesians 4:27

Neither give place to the devil.

2 Corinthians 10:3-4

For though we walk in the flesh, we do not war after the flesh: (for the weapons of our warfare are not carnal, but mighty through God to the pulling down of strong holds).

Once the strongholds have been demolished, you and your family can *"take captive every thought to make it obedient to Christ."* And thoughts which you submit to Jesus make you available to do the will of the Father, thereby enabling you to escape a life of iniquity.

First, however, you must acknowledge and then rid yourself of the iniquities of your forefathers. Again we can see how the Israelites did it:

Nehemiah 9:2

And the seed of Israel separated themselves from all strangers, and stood and confessed their sins, and the iniquities of their fathers.

Daniel 9:16

O Lord, according to all thy righteousness, I beseech thee, let thine anger and thy fury be turned away from thy city Jerusalem, thy holy mountain: because for our sins, and for the iniquities of our fathers, Jerusalem and thy people are become a reproach to all that are about us.

Jeremiah 14:20

We acknowledge, O Lord, our wickedness, and the iniquity of our fathers: for we have sinned against thee.

Psalm 119:133

Order my steps in thy word: and let not any iniquity have dominion over me.

Take the time to trace the iniquities that may have been passed down to current generations of your family and then deal with them decisively, using your spiritual weapons.

Be free in the name of Jesus and get ready to spread blessings to the coming generations.

Now, let me end the book as I began it: Are you living up to the level of your inner vision and potential? We all start out with big dreams and visions for the future. But, then, when the future becomes the present, it rarely lives up to the magnitude of our original dreams. God called us to do great things, to have great influence, and to change our world. What has been holding us back? Could it be generational curses? If so, I pray that this book has been a blessing to you and that you can now move forward into your glorious future.

I hope you will look forward to my next book on *Generational Blessings.*

OTHER BOOKS
BY
PROPHETESS JACKIE HAREWOOD

Sing Unto the Lord a New Song: An Introduction to Praise and Worship
(0-97-9712623-0-6)

The Violent Take It by Force
(978-1-934769-11-9)

Intercession Builds Bridges: Frequently Asked Questions About Intercession
(978-1-59872-909-2)

Overshadowed by the Almighty
(978-1-934769-99-7)

Ballistic Apostolic Prayer
(978-1-940461-55-7)

Learning to Use Your Greatest Weapon
(978-1-940461-56-4)

Warring with the Scriptures
(978-1-940461-73-1)

Make a Joyful Noise
(978-1-940461-74-8)

The Violent Take it by Force

Intercession Made Easy

Jackie Harewood

Overshadowed by the Almighty

Understanding the Phenomenon Known as "Being Slain in the Spirit"

With a special chapter entitled What Does God's Voice Sound Like?

Prophetess Jackie Harewood

Ballistic Apostolic Prayer

Jackie Harewood

Learning to Use Your Greatest Weapon

Prophetess Jackie Harewood

WARRING with the SCRIPTURES

Arm Yourself with Power-Packed Words to Reign in Victory

Prophetess Jackie Harewood

MAKE A JOYFUL NOISE

An Introduction to Praise and Worship

Prophetess Jackie Harewood

I Will Bless THEE

Discovering the Untapped Power of COVENANT

Apostle David Harewood

AUTHOR CONTACT PAGE

Prophetess Jackie Harewood
37041 Agnes Webb Avenue
Prairieville, LA 70769

jharewoodla@cox.net
(225) 772-4552

www.ingramcontent.com/pod-product-compliance
Lightning Source LLC
LaVergne TN
LVHW011330080426
835513LV00006B/276

* 9 7 8 1 9 4 0 4 6 1 7 9 3 *